JAMES & JUDE BIBLE STUDY

DISCOVER 40 PRACTICAL INSIGHTS FROM JESUS'S BROTHERS

40-DAY BIBLE STUDY SERIES
BOOK 11

PETER DEHAAN

James & Jude Bible Study: Discover 40 Practical Insights from Jesus's Brothers

Copyright © 2024 by Peter DeHaan.

40-Day Bible Study Series, Book 11

All rights reserved: No part of this book may be reproduced, disseminated, or transmitted in any form, by any means, or for any purpose, without the express written consent of the author or his legal representatives. The only exceptions are brief excerpts, and the cover image, for reviews or academic research. For permissions: peterdehaan.com/contact.

Unless otherwise noted, Scriptures taken from the Holy Bible, New International Version®, NIV®. Copyright © 1973, 1978, 1984, 2011 by Biblica, Inc. ™ Used by permission of Zondervan. All rights reserved worldwide. www.zondervan.com The "NIV" and "New International Version" are trademarks registered in the United States Patent and Trademark Office by Biblica, Inc.™

Library of Congress Control Number: 2024915461

Published by Rock Rooster Books, Grand Rapids, Michigan

ISBN:

- 979-8-88809-093-0 (e-book)
- 979-8-88809-094-7 (paperback)
- 979-8-88809-095-4 (hardcover)
- 979-8-88809-096-1 (audiobook)

Credits:

- Developmental editor: Julie Harbison
- Copy editor: Robyn Mulder
- Cover design: Fanderclai Design
- Author photo: Chelsie Jensen Photography

To Jim and Angie Byrne

Series by Peter DeHaan

40-Day Bible Study Series takes a fresh and practical look into Scripture, book by book.

Bible Character Sketches Series celebrates people in Scripture, from the well-known to the obscure.

Holiday Celebration Devotional Series rejoices in the holidays with Jesus.

Visiting Churches Series takes an in-person look at church practices and traditions to inform and inspire today's followers of Jesus.

Be the first to hear about Peter's new books and receive updates at PeterDeHaan.com/updates.

CONTENTS

James and Jude	1
The Letter Of James	5
Day 1: Pure Joy	7
Day 2: Ask God for Wisdom	11
Day 3: High and Low	15
Day 4: Persevere Under Trial	18
Day 5: The Source of Temptation	22
Bonus Content: God Does Not Change	26
Day 6: Be Quick to Listen	28
Day 7: Listen and Obey	31
Day 8: Pure and Faultless Religion	34
Day 9: Be Impartial	37
Day 10: Inherit the Kingdom	41
Day 11: Keep the Royal Law	44
Day 12: The Law Reveals Our Guilt	47
Day 13: Judgment versus Mercy	50
Day 14: Actionless Faith	53
Bonus Content: Even the Demons Believe	57
Day 15: Faith without Deeds Is Useless	59
Day 16: A Higher Standard	62
Day 17: Watch Your Words	65
Day 18: Tame the Tongue	69
Bonus Content: Double-Minded	73
Day 19: Live a Good Life	75
Day 20: Wisdom from Above	78
Day 21: Fights and Quarrels	83

Day 22: Spiritual Adultery	87
Bonus Content: James in the Old Testament	90
Day 23: Submit to God	92
Day 24: Watch What We Say	95
Day 25: If It's the Lord's Will	99
Day 26: Weep and Wail	102
Day 27: Be Patient	105
Bonus Content: Do Not Swear	108
Day 28: Pray	110
Day 29: Elijah's Example	114
Day 30: Bring Them Back	118
The Letter Of Jude	122
Day 31: Contend for the Faith	123
Day 32: Grace and Judgment	127
Day 33: Slander	131
Day 34: Woe to Them	134
Day 35: Blemishes	138
Day 36: Judge and Convict the Ungodly	142
Bonus Content: Ungodly	146
Day 37: Scoffers	148
Day 38: Pray in the Spirit	152
Day 39: Help Those in Need	156
Day 40: Praise Him	160
Books in the 40-Day Bible Study Series	164
For Small Groups, Sunday School, and Classes	166
If You're New to the Bible	168
About Peter DeHaan	171
Books by Peter DeHaan	173

JAMES AND JUDE

We view James and Jude as the authors of the books that bear their names. But who is James? Who is Jude? Let's look at what Scripture tells us.

James

There are several men named James in the New Testament (but none in the Old). The one we might best know is James, the brother of John and a disciple of Jesus. Yet King Herod arrests and executes James early in the book of Acts (Acts 12:1–2). That means this James would not have been alive to write this letter.

Two other men named James are the son of

Alphaeus and the father of Judas (Acts 1:13). As secondary characters, it's unlikely either wrote the letter of James.

One of Jesus's brothers, however, is James (Matthew 13:55). He's a fixture in the early church in Jerusalem (Acts 15:13) and becomes its leader after Peter flees to avoid imprisonment (Acts 21:18). It's this James, the brother of Jesus, who most likely writes the book that bears his name.

Yet he opens his letter with the humblest of greetings, saying he's a servant of Jesus Christ (James 1:1). It's as if his biological connection with the Savior of the world doesn't matter. What does matter is that he's God's servant.

Jude

The name Jude only appears once in the Bible, and it's in the opening of his letter (Jude 1:1). Like James, he identifies himself as a servant of Jesus Christ. In addition, he mentions he's a brother of James.

In Matthew 13:55, we learn that Jesus's brothers are James, Joseph, Simon, and Judas (Jude). Jude already revealed he's the brother of James.

We should understand Jude as an alternate

form of Judas. After Judas Iscariot betrays Jesus, who among Jesus's followers would want to go by the name Judas? I wouldn't. And who would be uneasy opening a letter from Judas—even though it's from a different man? It would certainly give me pause. Going by Jude instead of Judas makes sense.

Brothers

This means we have two books of the Bible written by Jesus's brothers. This is noteworthy for two reasons.

First, they didn't initially believe in him (John 7:5). They were understandably skeptical that the brother they grew up with could be God's son. Yet they eventually believe and identify as his servants. This is a dramatic transformation, from skeptics to followers.

Second, though Jesus's disciples spend three years with him, James and Jude have spent their entire life with him, until his death. This gives them a twenty, twenty-five, or even thirty-year history with Jesus. Therefore—outside of his mother Mary—James and Jude have known Jesus longer than anyone else in the early church. This makes their insights about him and his teachings even more profound.

Given all this, we'll do well to embrace and contemplate the words in these letters from James and Jude, servants of the Lord Jesus Christ.

Like James and Jude, should we consider ourselves servants of Jesus? How can we best serve our Lord and Savior?

[Discover more about another man who identifies as Jesus's servant in 1 Corinthians 4:1, Ephesians 3:7, and Philippians 1:1.]

THE LETTER OF JAMES
JAMES 1:1

James, a servant of God and of the Lord Jesus Christ, To the twelve tribes scattered among the nations: Greetings.
(James 1:1)

James writes to the twelve tribes scattered throughout the area. Saying *twelve tribes* suggests he's writing to Jewish Christians or Jewish believers. If so, does his letter apply to us as Gentiles (that is, non-Jews)? Yes! These believers are the early followers of Jesus, so by extension, a message to them then is a message to us now.

But not all versions of the Bible say *the twelve*

tribes. Other descriptors are *God's people* and *God's faithful*. This most certainly applies to us.

Let's discover all that James packs into his powerful letter of instruction and encouragement.

DAY 1: PURE JOY
JAMES 1:2–4

Consider it pure joy, my brothers and sisters, whenever you face trials of many kinds. (James 1:2)

After moving past the salutation of the letter, James opens with an oft-quoted verse about pure joy. What an exciting beginning! We all want joy. And pure joy—that is, joy at its finest—is even better.

Yet James connects this pure joy with facing trials. Hardships are something we'd all like to avoid. We don't even want to read about them. Yet James combines these two extremes.

First, we should consider joy as not being synonymous with happy, even though the dictionary uses one word as a possible descriptor of the other. Being happy is more superficial and temporary, whereas joy is deeper and transcendent. This is the joy James refers to.

When we encounter life's difficulties, we should embrace them with joy—with pure joy. We know that as we persevere through these challenges, we will become better for it. We grow, and we mature. We become stronger and more complete as a person, as a follower of Jesus. It sets us up to finish the race before us (2 Timothy 4:7).

What are these trials?

Trials of "many kinds" cover an array of ordeals. Rather than specify what they are, James leaves it up to us individually to determine. What looms as a hardship for one may not be a hardship for someone else. A burden that may test the faith of one person may be a non-issue for another.

Let's consider some kinds of trials we may face.

What first comes to mind is temptations. The temptation to sin is a huge trial for many. When we face temptation, we turn toward God and resist it (1 Corinthians 10:13). Each time we resist, we become stronger.

Another area that can produce trials comes from relationships. Some relationships present formidable challenges. This may occur at work, with neighbors, or from our own family. These can produce emotional distress. We must seek the Holy Spirit to guide us in navigating these difficulties in a God-honoring way. (If the threat is physical, we must first seek to keep ourselves safe.)

A third consideration is money, along with food, shelter, and the necessities of life. These provide another type of trial that many people face. Whether these come from within—poor decision-making—or from without, James wants us to confront it with pure joy. We know that as we seek God to persevere through it, we will mature in the process.

Each one of these scenarios can produce a crisis of faith. We pray for God to deliver us from our specific trial, but the answers may not come as fast as we'd like or in the way we wish. We may then question God and the confidence we place in him.

Our faith can also undergo a trial—a testing—when doubt forms in our minds. This can come from what other people say or when the enemy assaults us. It's not wrong to struggle in this area, but it is wrong to let this distress turn us from God. Instead, we should give our questions and our doubts over to him, trusting him to guide us through it as we seek him.

As we face these various trials, we should know that through the test we will develop perseverance and mature into who God wants us to become.

This should give us pure joy.

What trials do we face? How can we better embrace them with pure joy?

[Discover more about joy in Luke 6:22–23, John 15:10–12, Romans 14:17, and Galatians 5:22.]

DAY 2: ASK GOD FOR WISDOM
JAMES 1:5–8

If any of you lacks wisdom, you should ask God, who gives generously to all without finding fault, and it will be given to you. (James 1:5)

Another popular verse in the letter of James comes next. It's a personal favorite. James states that if we lack wisdom, we should ask God.

He's generous, without restrictions. He will give us wisdom. It's that simple.

There is, however, a caveat. When we ask for wisdom, we must believe that God will provide and not doubt. Doubt causes uncertainty, which James equates to an ocean wave tossing about. If we doubt, we shouldn't expect to receive anything from God, including wisdom. A person who doubts is double-minded. Their uncertainty offsets their confidence in receiving what they requested.

Suddenly the simple prayer of asking for wisdom and receiving it doesn't seem so easy.

Obviously, it's best to pray full of faith and without an ounce of doubt. Yet this doesn't mean that doubt automatically negates the effectiveness of our prayers.

Consider Peter. His faith in Jesus's command to come to him allows the disciple to walk on water. But when he takes his eyes off Jesus and looks at the physical environment around him, he doubts. He sinks. Yet Jesus rescues him, despite his doubt (Matthew 14:29–31).

Peter started his trip walking on water full of faith. He believed that through Jesus he could do the impossible. And he did—for a while. Yet, despite his initial success, doubt assaulted him and caused him to question what he was doing. That's when he faltered. But Jesus was there for him when he did. Jesus's reaction to Peter's uncertainty can comfort us when we struggle to fully believe.

Before we criticize Peter too heavily for his understandable doubt, remember that he was the only disciple with enough faith to get out of the boat. Instead of chastising him for a moment of doubt, we should celebrate him for his faith to act.

Another time, a father comes to Jesus. He asks the healer to drive out an evil spirit from his boy. The disciples had already tried and failed, so the dad may wonder whether Jesus can. The man conditions his request for healing with the tentative word *if*.

Jesus seems a bit insulted. He says anything is possible if we believe.

The man gives a most honest—and insightful—response. He says, "I do believe! Help me overcome my unbelief." Then Jesus heals the boy (Mark 9:17–27).

This story should provide us with much comfort when in the presence of doubt. This father had an element of belief paired with nonbelief. The two coexisted as a jumbled conflict in his mind. Yet he implicitly turned his doubts over to Jesus. And that was it.

We can learn from this example when we ask God for wisdom. We ask in faith, and we ask him to take away our doubts. When we do, we can expect to receive wisdom, just as the man received healing for his son.

What is our reaction to doubt? Have we asked Jesus to take our doubts away?

[Discover more about wisdom in James 3:13–17.]

DAY 3: HIGH AND LOW
JAMES 1:9–11

Believers in humble circumstances ought to take pride in their high position. (James 1:9)

A quick read of today's passage may cause us to shake our heads in confusion. We may breeze past it to get to something easier to understand and more comforting. But don't do that.

This passage talks about being high and low. It mentions humility contrasted with pride. We must slow down and contemplate its words to embrace its meaning. As we do, we'll gain insights of worth that point us to eternity.

This passage places people into two categories.

One is those who have little, and the other is those who have much, with the two contrasted to each other.

Believers who have little in this world are of humble circumstances. They lack money, power, and prestige. Society views them as inconsequential, as low. Yet this is not how God esteems them. As followers of Jesus, they have a high standing with him and through him in the spiritual realm. Therefore, they'll do well to not focus on their less-than-ideal physical state. Instead, they look forward to their future with Jesus in heaven. This is something to celebrate.

The opposite is those who have much in this world. They are rich. They occupy places of power and bask in prestige. Society esteems them, elevating them in importance. They have a high standing in this world.

Yet they shouldn't place their trust—their confidence—in possessions or station. It's temporary. It won't last. What they've accomplished and what they've accumulated will fade and disappear.

In the end, they—along with everyone else—will die. Their money can't save them. Only Jesus can.

Jesus warns the people not to stockpile money

and possessions here on earth. It can be destroyed or stolen. Instead, they should seek to store treasures in heaven (Matthew 6:19–21). What they place there will last forever. No one can take it away.

Jesus ends by saying that where their treasure is, their heart will follow.

Where have we stored our treasures? What can we do to look beyond our present situation here on earth to focus on our future in heaven?

[Discover more about the folly of earthly pursuits in Matthew 16:25–26 and Luke 12:16–21.]

DAY 4: PERSEVERE UNDER TRIAL
JAMES 1:12

Blessed is the one who perseveres under trial because, having stood the test, that person will receive the crown of life that the Lord has promised to those who love him. (James 1:12)

In "Day 1: Pure Joy," we discussed trials and perseverance. James returns to this topic. It's as if he wants to make sure we don't miss his point. He tells us a second time to make sure we get it.

He encourages us to persevere when undergoing trials. He equates this to a test. When we persevere amid difficulty, we pass the test. Then we'll receive the "crown of life."

What is the *crown of life*? A common understanding is that it refers to our future in heaven with Jesus. Yet if we don't persevere—if we don't pass the testing of our trials—will we not receive our crown? It's a worrisome thought. But remember that salvation is a gift from God that we can't earn (Ephesians 2:8–9). Therefore, even if we fail to persevere under our trials, we won't lose our right standing with God.

Given this, consider that the *crown of life* is something for us to offer to our Lord in worship of him in heaven, just like the twenty-four elders do in Revelation 4:9–11. As such, if we don't have a crown, we'll have nothing to give to God. But we will still be with him regardless.

The Bible is full of colorful characters who persevere when undergoing trials. Consider Abraham, Job, Daniel, Jeremiah, Hosea, and many more. Yet Joseph may stand out as our prime example.

His older brothers hate him because he's their father's favorite son. When Joseph is seventeen, his brothers throw him into a pit, intent on killing him. Instead, they sell him as a slave, earning a bit of money in the process.

While in bondage, Joseph ends up serving Potiphar and conducts himself well. Yet he's falsely accused of sexual assault and ends up in jail. He languishes in prison. Again, he conducts himself well and is elevated to oversee the prisoners, although still incarcerated himself.

While in prison, Joseph interprets a dream for a fellow prisoner who is later released. But the man forgets to intercede for Joseph, despite his promise to do so.

Two years later, the man remembers Joseph. Pharaoh releases Joseph from prison to interpret his dream. Joseph even recommends a wise course of action. The pharaoh appoints Joseph to implement his plan, making him the second most powerful person in the nation of Egypt (Genesis 37–41).

Joseph is thirty when this happens. This means he spent thirteen years enduring a series of trials (age seventeen to thirty). Yet he persevered. He passed the tests. Every one of them. This prepares him to ascend to a position of power and save the nation—and his family—during a seven-year famine.

Joseph's example should encourage us to persevere in our trials, regardless of how long they might last. If he can do it, so can we.

May we—through God's grace—pass our test and receive our crown.

How do our trials compare to Joseph's? How well do we do to persevere under hardship?

[Discover more about perseverance in Romans 5:3–4, 1 Corinthians 13:6–7, Hebrews 10:36, 2 Peter 1:5–7, and Revelation 2:2–3.]

DAY 5: THE SOURCE OF TEMPTATION
JAMES 1:13–18

When tempted, no one should say, "God is tempting me." For God cannot be tempted by evil, nor does he tempt anyone.
(James 1:13)

James states unequivocally that God does not tempt us, and we should not claim that he does. Just as God is impervious to evil's temptation, he likewise doesn't tempt anyone.

Instead, temptation comes from within. There's a progression we must guard against. It starts with an evil desire, an enticement, which forms in our mind. We entertain thoughts of sinning. Next, we yield to it, and then we commit the sin.

James & Jude Bible Study

James likens this to biology. Just as human conception gives birth to life, our minds conceive desire, which gives birth to sin. And sin leads to death.

Fortunately for us, Jesus offers us a prescription to counter sin's death grip on us. Though we deserve to die for our mistakes, God gives us eternal life through Jesus (Romans 6:23).

When we consider that God does not tempt us, however, we may recall some Old Testament examples that seem to counter this.

Consider Job. He certainly faces the temptation to turn his back on God amid his turmoil. His wife even encourages him to do so (Job 2:9). But he does not. His afflictions—and the temptations that result—do not come from God. Instead, they come from Satan. In addition, God mercifully places limits on Satan's ability to torment Job (Job 1:12 and Job 2:6). In doing so, God protects him from the full fury of the enemy's assault.

Next, we read about God hardening hearts, such as the pharoah (Exodus 4:21). This is a case of God exercising his sovereign power to accomplish his will for his people. But he is not tempting the Egyptian ruler to sin. Pharoah does that on his own.

In similar fashion, we see God, angry against

the nation of Israel, inciting David to take a census of his army. This again is to accomplish his sovereign purpose. Joab even tries to talk David out of it. But the king won't listen to his commander. Afterward, David becomes conscious-stricken over what he did. He confesses his sin and asks God to take it away from him. God does, but there are consequences (2 Samuel 24:1–17).

We must consider these accounts carefully and hold them loosely. In these, we see a tension between God's actions and the assertion that temptation does not come from him. We should note that each account is descriptive, while James's teaching is direct.

The temptation to sin does not come from God but from within. It's up to us to decide what to do with it. Do we give in to it, or do we resist it?

Paul teaches that God will not let us face temptation beyond our ability to bear it. Furthermore, when we face temptation, God will show us a way out so we can prevail (1 Corinthians 10:13).

With God's help, we can overcome temptation.

Who do we blame when we face temptation? What steps can

we take to resist the impulse to sin and instead have victory over it?

[Discover more about temptation in Matthew 26:41 and Hebrews 4:15.]

BONUS CONTENT: GOD DOES NOT CHANGE

Every good and perfect gift is from above, coming down from the Father of the heavenly lights, who does not change like shifting shadows. (James 1:17)

Wrapping up his discussion about temptation and sin, James slides in an acknowledgment that God does not change.

He uses the image of shadows to illustrate his point. As the sun moves across the sky, the shade it produces shifts throughout the day. The shadow moves little by little, nearly imperceptibly, but it makes a full sweep from dawn to dusk.

Our Lord is not like that.

God does not change. We can rely on him to be the same throughout the day and throughout our life. He wants what's best for us and blesses us.

That will never change. We can count on it.

Though God does not change, how has our view of him shifted over time? How does God's unchanging nature give us confidence today in what he said in the Bible thousands of years ago?

[Discover more about God's unchanging nature in Psalm 55:19, Malachi 3:6, and Hebrews 13:8.]

DAY 6: BE QUICK TO LISTEN
JAMES 1:19–21

Everyone should be quick to listen, slow to speak and slow to become angry. (James 1:19)

An old saying contains much wisdom: "God gave us two ears and one mouth. Therefore, we should listen twice as much as we talk." I wonder if this is the author's astute way of paraphrasing today's verse.

James writes that everyone—which includes you and me—should be quick to listen. We should also be slow to speak. Along with that, we should be slow to become angry.

It's not wrong to become angry. Sometimes anger is justified, but the key is to not sin because of it (Ephesians 4:26). Yet, for most people, anger results in sin. For this reason, the wise solution is to avoid the anger in the first place. This starts with listening first and being slow to speak.

Many in today's world, however, ignore James's wise advice, turning it on its head. They are slow to listen, if they even listen at all. They are quick to speak, often without thinking before they talk. Anger surrounds their words, what they do, and who they are.

We've all met people like this. By their countenance, we know they're angry. They reveal this without saying a word. It's who they are and how they carry themselves. When they speak, their anger intensifies.

Instead, they should follow James's sage advice to be quick to listen. We should all endeavor to do this.

Only when we listen can we understand. Only then should we entertain the idea of speaking. This is a sure way to keep our anger in check and the sin that can result from it far away.

James writes that anger cannot produce the God-honoring righteousness he desires. Notice how James contrasts the specific area of anger with the general category of righteousness.

Building on this idea of producing righteousness, he advises we get rid of our moral filth and proclivity toward evil. He reminds the twelve tribes—and us—of the salvation message they received. With humility, we should accept it as a seed planted within us and allow it to grow.

As followers of Jesus, an unrighteous anger has no place in our lives. We should seek his strength to move away from it.

This starts when we focus on listening before we talk.

How well do we do at listening before speaking? If others characterize us as an angry person, what should we do about it?

[Discover more about anger in 1 Corinthians 13:5 and Colossians 3:8.]

DAY 7: LISTEN AND OBEY
JAMES 1:22–25

Do not merely listen to the word, and so deceive yourselves. Do what it says. (James 1:22)

Building upon the theme of listening, James says that when it comes to God's word, we must do more than just listen. We need to put into practice what we hear. We need to apply it to our lives. It's imperative that we obey it.

We can best understand James's use of *the word* as referring to the Scripture of the day. Yet some versions of the Bible render this phrase as God's teaching or his message. We can receive this meaning of *the word* through God's written Word, the Bible, along with God's spoken word through the Holy Spirit.

Though most of us today can read the Bible, two thousand years ago, few people had that luxury. Not all could read, and only some had a copy of the text. Instead, they listened as others read it to them.

Today, we can both read and hear the Word of God. But regardless of how we receive it, if we just listen and don't apply it, we deceive ourselves into thinking we've accomplished something worthwhile. We haven't.

To learn, we must listen and then do what we've heard (or read). For example, if we listen to a tutorial on how to complete a task, we can comprehend it. But until we do it—putting into practice what we've heard—the information we took in accomplishes nothing.

We must listen, and we must do. Otherwise, what we heard makes no difference in our lives or the lives of others. This applies to both tutorials and, more importantly, to God's Word.

Hearing but not doing is like looking at our face in the mirror. Though we see our likeness for a moment, the image vanishes once we walk away. It is gone.

So, too, is God's Word when we listen and don't

put what we've heard into action. We must listen, and then we must obey.

How often do we listen to or read God's Word? More importantly, how well do we apply what we've heard or read?

[Discover more about obedience in Luke 11:28, John 8:51, and 1 John 2:5.]

DAY 8: PURE AND FAULTLESS RELIGION
JAMES 1:26–27

Religion that God our Father accepts as pure and faultless is this: to look after orphans and widows in their distress and to keep oneself from being polluted by the world. (James 1:27)

James opened his letter by writing about pure joy. Now he talks about pure religion. I'm always a bit put off by the word religion. I don't want religion. I want relationship—with God, my Creator and my Savior.

To me, religion rings of hypocrisy, of people who wander far off track from what God intended for them. It was religious people who crucified Jesus, and it's religious people today who misrepresent him to a world that needs him. Their religion is static and dead. It means little and accomplishes nothing.

Yet, this isn't the type of religion James talks about. He clarifies this version of it as pure religion, as faultless. The pure and faultless religion Father God wants us to have addresses two areas.

First, a pure and faultless religion looks after orphans and widows in their distress. It attends to their needs. It helps them. In that day, widows and orphans were the poorest of the poor. They had no one to advocate for them and no one to provide. They struggled in poverty, scrounging to survive from one day to the next.

Throughout Scripture, we see that God has a heart for widows and orphans (specifically the fatherless). He wants us to have a heart for them as well, to help them in their need. Paul, in writing to Timothy, gives some practical advice in this area. It starts with our family (1 Timothy 5:3–8).

Caring for widows and orphans addresses the needs of others. It's one way to exhibit pure and faultless religion.

The second aspect of pure and faultless religion is internal. It's keeping ourselves from being polluted by the world, from being corrupted by its negative influences. It's fighting worldly pressures that pull us away from God and push us toward the evil he opposes.

The opposite of worldly living is right living or righteousness. We should want to live right because it's the appropriate thing to do. This isn't to earn our salvation, but it's our response to it.

Living a righteous life is our way of thanking Jesus for saving us. It is pure and faultless religion.

What is a practical way we can help widows and orphans today? What can we do to keep ourselves from being polluted by the world?

[Discover more about being worldly in 1 Corinthians 3:1–3 and Titus 2:11–13.]

DAY 9: BE IMPARTIAL
JAMES 2:1–4

Believers in our glorious Lord Jesus Christ must not show favoritism. (James 2:1)

James writes that we are not to show favoritism. On the surface, this appears as a call to be impartial and not differentiate between people in any way. Yet it's an overreach to claim this as a universal truth that applies in all circumstances. It is not.

To better understand what James means in not showing favoritism, let's look at the context of this passage. His key distinction comes from the motives behind our actions. If we do something with evil intent, it is wrong. This implies that sometimes showing favoritism is okay. One example might be putting family first.

If our motivation to treat one person differently than another comes from a selfish desire or worldly perspective, we must stop. In doing so, we discriminate and judge others with evil thoughts (James 2:4). This displeases Jesus and disrespects them.

James's example is treating a wealthy person with respect and dismissing a poor person at our meetings. Today, *at our meetings* means at church. We perceive a person who is well-off as someone who can donate much, while a person who is poor may only give a little. Remember, Jesus praises the widow who only gives two coins (Luke 21:1–3). This example shows discriminating between people through wrong motives.

A parallel consideration occurs when someone held in high esteem comes to church. They wield power or influence in society, which we desire to benefit from. We fawn over them, all the while ignoring someone who lacks a distinguished standing. We must avoid this type of favoritism.

I've seen people take this verse about favoritism out of context. They often apply it to their ministers and church leaders, insisting everyone should have equal access and treatment. They see others who enjoy a closer relationship with these leaders, so they heap on criticism for not receiving the same attention.

For insight into this situation, let's look at Jesus. Jesus had thousands who heard him preach. He had a much smaller number who followed him. From them he picked twelve to serve as disciples. From the twelve, he chose three—Peter, James, and John—to serve as his inner circle.

Isn't this an example of favoritism?

No. It's an example of being strategic with a God-honoring intent. Jesus favored those who were receptive to his teaching, who could grow in their faith and become leaders themselves. He invested in them more than others because of their potential to spread his good news after he was gone.

This is the opposite of showing favoritism with evil intent, of wrongly discriminating and judging. Instead, it's favoring others with a God-honoring focus to grow his kingdom.

When have we shown favoritism with the wrong motivation?

How can we rightly be strategic in who we surround ourselves with?

[Discover more about favoritism in Leviticus 19:15 and Galatians 2:6.]

DAY 10: INHERIT THE KINGDOM
JAMES 2:5–7

Has not God chosen those who are poor in the eyes of the world to be rich in faith and to inherit the kingdom he promised those who love him? (James 2:5)

James encourages us when he says those who are poor in the eyes of the world are rich in faith (see "Day 3: High and Low"). They will inherit the kingdom, while those who are rich in this world will find it difficult to enter God's kingdom (Luke 18:25). Despite this, it's still possible for them to inherit the kingdom.

James says *inherit the kingdom*. He doesn't say *earn* it. We can't earn our salvation. It's a gift God gives us (Ephesians 2:8–9). We receive it because of who we are.

As God's children, we receive an inheritance from him. But how are we God's children? The Bible gives us two images to consider. The first is adoption, and the second is marriage.

Adoption is a beautiful act. Adoptive parents choose the children they adopt. It's intentional. As God's adopted children, he selected us. He chose us. Isn't that amazing?

Paul writes that when we receive God's Spirit we're adopted into his family. In doing so, we become his sons and daughters (Romans 8:15). Our adoption was his plan from the beginning (Ephesians 1:4–6). Through our adoption into his family, we become children of God and his heirs, co-heirs with Jesus (Romans 8:17). As heirs, we receive eternal life from him (Titus 3:7).

Next, consider marriage.

Jesus talks about the bridegroom and his bride, implying he's the groom, and his followers are his bride.

John the Baptist testifies that he came to pave the way for the Messiah, who is Jesus, the bridegroom. We, as the bride, belong to the groom (John 3:27–29).

James & Jude Bible Study

John later reiterates this in his epic vision, which culminates with a future wedding of bridegroom and bride. Jesus is the Lamb, and we are his bride (Revelation 21:1–4, 21:9, and 22:17).

As Christ's bride, we become God's children through our spiritual marriage to his Son. God has one Son, and through our marriage to his Son, we, too, become God's children.

As God's kids, we are heirs of all he has. This includes the gift of spending eternity with him.

But someone must die before the heirs can receive their inheritance. The death has already occurred. It happened when Jesus died for us on the cross. Through his death we receive his inheritance, the kingdom he promised.

What do we think about marrying into or being adopted into God's family? Are we ready to receive the inheritance he promised?

[Discover more about being adopted into God's family in Romans 8:23, Galatians 4:4–6, and Ephesians 1:4–6.]

DAY 11: KEEP THE ROYAL LAW
JAMES 2:8–9

If you really keep the royal law found in Scripture, "Love your neighbor as yourself," you are doing right. (James 2:8)

The unfamiliar phrase *royal law* does not occur anywhere else in the Bible, so we can't use Scripture to help us understand what it means here. But given the context, we will do well to think of it as an important law from God, or one of his chief commands. This instruction to love others as much as ourselves comes from the Old Testament law, as found in Leviticus 19:18.

In the New Testament, when asked what's the greatest commandment, Jesus says it's loving God above all else. And the second greatest one is to love our neighbors as much as we love ourselves (Matthew 22:36–40 and Mark 12:29–31). These stand as the greatest commandments from God's royal law.

James's emphasis on the importance of loving others in his letter isn't to elevate it over the primacy of loving God (Deuteronomy 6:5). Rather, he talks about it here because his text focuses on our relationship with others, specifically regarding wrongly showing favoritism (James 2:1–4).

When it comes to showing favoritism, the command to love others as much as ourselves serves as an astute guideline.

Just as we wouldn't want one person to elevate someone else over us, we shouldn't do it to others. The opposite also applies. Just as we wouldn't want someone to dismiss us based on our worldly value, we shouldn't do it to others.

In both cases, we should treat other people as we want to be treated.

Yet when we don't do this, we show favoritism. It is wrong. It is a sin. And we break the law. James expands on this in the verses that follow, which we'll cover in tomorrow's reading.

But for today, let's focus on the key lesson of loving others as much as we love ourselves. This is the sure prescription to protect us from wrongly showing favoritism to others.

What do we need to change in our lives to better love others as much as we love ourselves? How can loving God above all else help us better love others?

[Discover more about love in 1 Corinthians 13:4–7.]

DAY 12: THE LAW REVEALS OUR GUILT
JAMES 2:10–11

Whoever keeps the whole law and yet stumbles at just one point is guilty of breaking all of it. (James 2:10)

Having just told us that when we wrongly show favoritism, we break the law, James expands on this by talking about the law in general. If we falter over just one element of it, we're guilty of breaking it all.

He gives us two examples to consider. These are weighty issues. He addresses adultery and murder, which the Ten Commandments prohibit (Exodus 20:1–17 and Deuteronomy 5:7–21).

In considering adultery and murder, I hope you can say you've not broken either one. But lest we become smug over this, let's consider what Jesus says on these topics.

In his esteemed sermon, which we often call the Sermon on the Mount, Jesus talks about the Old Testament command to not commit adultery. The teacher then expands on what this means. He says that if anyone looks at a woman with lust, he's already committed adultery with her in his heart (Matthew 5:27–28). Yet lust is not solely the domain of men. Women can lust too. When we lust for another, we commit adultery with them in our hearts. We are guilty of sin. This is true even if we don't physically give in to the temptation and follow through.

Jesus likewise addresses murder. He says that anyone who is angry with another person is likewise guilty (Matthew 5:21–22). Whenever our anger causes us to lose control, we are guilty of sin, just as if we committed murder.

To understand this on a deeper level, we must know what the law says, which we find in the Old Testament. We must also grasp what the law intends, which Jesus reveals in the New Testament.

The law in the Old Testament details God's standard for right living. And it's a high standard, which no one can fully realize. James confirms this when he says whoever falters in just one area is guilty, just as guilty as if they had broken every single rule.

It matters not if we come up short by a little or a lot, we still miss meeting God's high expectations. Being mostly good is not good enough. We still fail.

Fortunately, Jesus offers us a better way. When he died on the cross, it served as a sacrificial death that addresses all our sins, both past and future. When we trust Jesus and follow him, through faith, he makes us right with Father God. This is something the Old Testament law can only point to.

Have we trusted Jesus to make us right with Father God? How should we react when we feel guilty over the mistakes we've made?

[Discover more about adultery in Mark 10:2–12. Read more about anger in Ephesians 4:26.]

DAY 13: JUDGMENT VERSUS MERCY
JAMES 2:12–13

Speak and act as those who are going to be judged by the law that gives freedom. (James 2:12)

It's interesting that James tells us to behave as if we will face judgment under the law. But aren't we saved by faith and not by what we do (Ephesians 2:8–9)? Correct. Then what we do shouldn't matter. Or does it?

It's true there's nothing we can do to earn our salvation. We receive it in faith and not through our actions. This is because our deeds will always fall short of meeting Father God's exacting standards.

Yet once we receive our right standing with Papa through Jesus, we should *want* to change our behavior as an act of gratitude. It's a way of saying "thank you," of showing ourselves worthy of receiving the ultimate gift of salvation.

It's important to note that we don't have to change our behavior first. But we should, however, want to do better afterward. In this way, we work *out* our salvation (Philippians 2:12–13). This is not to work *for* our salvation so that we can receive it. It's to work *out* what we already have.

We do this by aligning our behavior with the law that gives us freedom, the law that gives liberty. But this is confusing. Fully adhering to the Old Testament law—as if that were possible—will indeed give us freedom. But our inability to do so keeps us from being free.

Yet the law points to a better way through Jesus. Jesus does, in fact, free us. He liberates us from the weight of our sins, our shortcomings. In this way, the law gives freedom, albeit indirectly, when it points us to Jesus.

The law demands judgment. Jesus offers mercy. I repeat, the law demands judgment, but Jesus offers mercy.

In the same way as Jesus offers us mercy, we should extend it to others. If we can't do this, it suggests we haven't received his mercy ourselves.

Moreover, if we insist on judgment without mercy, we cannot receive mercy.

Mercy overcomes judgment.

What do we think about changing our behavior in response to what Jesus did for us? How well do we do in offering mercy to others, as well as to ourselves?

[Discover more about mercy in Matthew 5:7, Luke 10:30–37, and Romans 11:30–32. Read more about judgment in Matthew 12:35–37 and Luke 6:37.)

DAY 14: ACTIONLESS FAITH
JAMES 2:14–18

What good is it, my brothers and sisters, if someone claims to have faith but has no deeds? Can such faith save them?
(James 2:14)

James opens this passage by asking if faith without action accomplishes anything. He'll return to this in a few verses, but for the moment, he gives a hypothetical question to contemplate.

Envision someone coming to us and asking for food or clothes. We raise our hand and offer them a blessing: "May you feel peace, stay warm, and eat well." Then we leave without addressing their needs. What does this accomplish?

We may have faith that God will provide for them, but if we don't back it up with action, it means little. Our faith is dead.

Yes, sometimes a person in need simply wants to receive a blessing. This is enough for them.

Other times, they merely need someone to listen. They don't want anyone to fix their problem. They just want to be heard. By sharing their concern, they lessen the weight they carry, and they leave satisfied.

A third scenario is when people seek prayer, wanting us to intercede for them. They prayed for God to provide, and now they ask us to join them in their request. We pray, which encourages them.

Yet blessing, listening, and praying should not be our default position when we see someone with a physical need. We should seek to address it. Blessing, listening, and praying should serve as secondary actions.

As we seek to help people meet their physical needs, we should do so with Holy Spirit discernment. We should know that sometimes what they ask for is not what they need. Consider Peter and John when the lame man asks for money. Instead of giving him what he requests, Peter heals him (Acts

James & Jude Bible Study

3:1–10). This addresses the man's genuine need but not his request.

Other times people ask for help, but they aren't specific. We shouldn't assume we know what they need. Too many times I've seen well-meaning people give aid that isn't helpful and fails to address the person's actual need.

Instead, we should ask what they want. Jesus does this when a blind man calls out to him for mercy (Luke 18:35–43).

Jesus says, "What do you want me to do for you?"

The man answers directly. "I want to see."

Then Jesus heals him.

A final consideration is to make sure that our help—such as giving money—doesn't enable them to persist in the same predicament. The better solution is to help them move from an untenable situation to a more realistic one.

For example, a person who doesn't earn enough money to pay rent doesn't need rent money. They'll just be in the same predicament next month. Instead, we should help them find a better-paying job or suggest that they move to a less expensive place.

Yet in all of this, our first inclination when

someone comes to us with a physical need should be to see what we can do to help them.

This is how we put our faith into action.

In what ways have we failed to put our faith into action? When have we tried to help someone but did it the wrong way?

[Discover more about faith in action in Hebrews 11:7–16.]

BONUS CONTENT: EVEN THE DEMONS BELIEVE

You believe that there is one God. Good! Even the demons believe that—and shudder. (James 2:19)

To add weight to the idea of faith without works—and give us astute insight—James talks about belief. His audience believes in God, and that's a good thing. It's commendable.

Yet he wisely points out that the demons believe too. Their belief causes them to shudder, whereas our belief should cause us to be in awe. The point, however, is that both we and they believe in God.

Mere belief is not enough.

That's why belief—like faith—must accompany

action for it to mean anything. Otherwise, we may not be much better off than the demons who likewise believe.

This is a serious thought to consider.

How does our belief in God differ from the demons who likewise believe? Does our belief in God cause us to be in awe or to shudder?

[Discover more about being in awe of God in Matthew 9:8, Luke 5:26, and Hebrews 12:28–29.]

DAY 15: FAITH WITHOUT DEEDS IS USELESS
JAMES 2:20–26

Do you want evidence that faith without deeds is useless?
(James 2:20)

James has shown us the folly of claiming we have faith but not backing it up by what we do. He then taught us that even the demons believe in God. *Belief* is a synonym for faith. Obviously, belief alone is insufficient.

To make sure we don't miss his point that our faith—and belief—requires action if it is to mean anything, he gives us the examples of two people to illustrate his point. One we readily grasp, while the other comes as a surprise. Who are these two people? Abraham and Rahab.

First, consider Abraham. God tells Abraham to take his son Isaac and sacrifice him as a burnt offering (Genesis 22:1–19). What a horrific thought.

Isaac is the long-awaited son God promised to Abraham and Sarah, given to them in their old age and well past their childbearing years. He's also their only child. If he dies, God's promise to bless Abraham with many descendants dies with Isaac.

In faith, Abraham intends to do exactly what God told him to do. This is despite the torment he surely faces over the thought of killing his only son.

Abraham, Isaac, and two servants leave the next day. They take wood for the fire with them. Isaac asks about a lamb for the burnt offering, not realizing his father intends for him to be the offering. Abraham simply says, "The Lord will provide the lamb."

With Isaac bound and lying on the altar, Abraham grabs his knife to slay his only son. At the last minute, an angel stops him. It was a test, and Abraham passes. He spots a ram caught in a thicket. He sacrifices the ram instead of Isaac.

Why did God provide a ram instead of the lamb that Abraham expected? The lamb comes later. It is Jesus. When Abraham proclaims that God will provide a lamb for the sacrifice, he prophetically looks forward to Jesus and his sacrifice for everyone throughout time.

Next, we shift our attention from the expected example of Abraham to the unexpected example of Rahab (Joshua 2:1–11). Rahab is a prostitute. She isn't even Jewish; she's a foreigner. Yet she believes, and her actions confirm it.

When Joshua sends two spies to learn about the land they need to conquer, especially the city of Jericho, they encounter Rahab. Rahab tells them she knows God has given them the land. She professes her confidence in him. Beyond this, she commits treason against her own people to protect the two spies and allow them to escape. In doing so, she puts her faith into action.

How can the faith of Abraham encourage us today? What does the celebration of Rahab for her faith teach us about God's perspective and who he esteems?

[Discover more about Abraham in Hebrews 11:17–19. Read more about Rahab in Hebrews 11:31.]

DAY 16: A HIGHER STANDARD
JAMES 3:1–2

Not many of you should become teachers, my fellow believers, because you know that we who teach will be judged more strictly. (James 3:1)

Many of us would like to teach others about God, the Bible, and faith. This may be formally through sermons on Sunday morning or teaching at conferences and seminars. We can also teach in a volunteer capacity to a Sunday school class, youth group, or Bible study meeting. Last is teaching through writing books and blog posts, like I do.

Though teaching others about Jesus is a noble pursuit, with the potential for God-honoring results, we must proceed with care. As James warns, we shouldn't all become teachers.

This seems counterintuitive. Yet he explains his rationale. Teachers face stricter judgment. God holds them to a higher standard, and rightly so.

Most students view their teachers with high esteem. Right or wrong, they look up to them. If a teacher falters—*when* a teacher falters, for we're all human—their failure will ripple through those who sit under their instruction. Some may follow their error, while others may have their faith shaken. In the most extreme situation, a disillusioned student will walk away from God, never to return.

These are all somber reasons for teachers to exercise care in what they do and the example they set. Yet these wise warnings go beyond the focus of James's letter. His chief concern isn't what these teachers do, but it's what they say. We see this in the verse that follows his advice that not many should become teachers.

There are many ways that we can stumble, and we all do. But what we say rises as more important. If we master our tongue and never falter in what we say, James proclaims us as perfect.

Since we know we'll fall short of perfection here on earth, we shouldn't consider James's declaration of *perfect* as literal. We're better to treat it as an overstatement to emphasize his point.

Even so, if we can control our tongue, we can keep our whole body in check. This applies to both teachers and to everyone else. That's you, and that's me.

What should be our attitude toward our teachers? Given James's stern warning, should we aspire to teach others?

[Discover more about the qualifications of leaders in 1 Timothy 3:1–13.]

DAY 17: WATCH YOUR WORDS
JAMES 3:3–6

The tongue is a small part of the body, but it makes great boasts. (James 3:5)

Building on his teaching about controlling what we say, James gives us three examples to illustrate his point. These are a bit in a horse's mouth, a rudder to steer a ship, and a spark that burns a forest.

A bit is an essential part of a horse's harness. It goes in their mouth, from one side to the other. It's not so tight as to cause pain, but it's snug enough to get the horse's attention. A rein attaches to each side of the bit. When the rider pulls on the left rein, it applies pressure to the horse's left cheek. In response, the horse turns its head in that direction to ease the discomfort. And where its head points, the body follows. To go the opposite way, the rider pulls on the other rein. Though the bit is small compared to the much larger horse, it controls where the animal goes.

In similar fashion, a small rudder on the back of a ship can direct the entire craft, according to the captain's wishes. It seems strange for such a small device to control such a large vessel, but that's how it works.

The third example is how a small spark can turn into a flame and burn down an entire forest. Though it starts small, almost insignificant, it can inflict widespread damage that no one can undo.

In these analogies, our tongues are like a horse's bit, a ship's rudder, and a tiny spark, controlling or destroying something much bigger than it. Through these illustrations, we see the effect our words—uttered by our tiny tongue—can have on others. Each can affect much. And like the spark that burns down the forest, once words leave our mouths, we can't take them back.

In this way, the tongue is a fire. It stands as one of our body's most evil parts, capable of corrupting our whole being, as if setting our life on fire with the fire of hell.

Consider Korah in the Bible. He, along with Dathan, Abiram, and On, opposes Moses, thereby rebelling against God. Their tongues set this in motion through the words they say. They claim Moses has gone too far, that everyone is holy, and that God is with them.

This verbal complaint starts as a small spark that fans into a fire. In their case, the fire is literal and comes from God. It consumes Korah's 250 followers as they offer incense, which God's law prohibits them from doing. As judgment for Korah and his three associates, the earth opens, consuming them, their families, and their possessions (Numbers 16:1–35).

This happened because they didn't control their tongues.

When does our tongue get us in trouble? What can we do to better guard what we say?

[Discover more about the tongue in Psalm 5:9,

Proverbs 10:19, and 1 Peter 3:10. Read what our tongue should do in Romans 14:11.]

DAY 18: TAME THE TONGUE
JAMES 3:7–12

No human being can tame the tongue. It is a restless evil, full of deadly poison. (James 3:8)

James told us about the dangers of the tongue. He started by warning teachers of the importance of controlling what they say. Then he expanded it to include everyone, equating our words to a spark that can start a fire and burn an entire forest.

This leaves us with the motivation to tame our tongue.

Indeed, we tame animals. Every animal is wild by nature, with some easier to tame than others. But we can control them all, at least to some degree. If we can tame animals, surely, we can tame the tongue. Right? Not so fast!

James states directly that no human can tame the tongue. No one. Not you, and not me. No one, at least no human being. This means that God can. With God all things are possible. Jesus himself says so. He states that what's impossible for us is possible with God (Luke 18:27). Another time he says to the man struggling with doubt that everything is possible if we believe (Mark 9:23).

Given the reality of our own limitations and the truth of God's power, we are wise to turn our tongue—and the words we say—over to God.

Yet we must also do our part. Just as we wouldn't ask God to help us lose weight and then not diet, so too with taming our tongue.

We should ask God to grant us control over our words, and then do our part. This isn't because he needs our help. It's because he may not be so inclined to answer our request if we aren't willing to even try.

Here are some areas to consider:

If we utter words we shouldn't say when we're angry, what can we do to avoid getting angry in the first place or not sinning when we do? (Ephesians 4:26).

Perhaps we say things we shouldn't when we're around a certain person or group. Maybe we need to avoid them or limit contact. Alternately, we can develop a plan to keep our words in check when in their presence.

Other people struggle to speak wisely when in front of a group of people or the center of everyone's attention. Again, seek to avoid those circumstances, and devise a plan to best deal with the situation.

The opposite is people who struggle with their words when around family or in private settings.

Of course, in each one of these circumstances we're not left to our own strength to control our words. Instead, we can seek God's help to be victorious when we encounter each one of these situations.

Though we cannot tame our tongue, that doesn't mean we shouldn't try. We should do what we can and turn the rest over to God.

Which of these scenarios do we need to guard against? How can we turn our tongue over to God and trust him to tame it?

[Discover more about self-control in Galatians 5:22–24 and 2 Peter 1:3–8.]

BONUS CONTENT: DOUBLE-MINDED

Out of the same mouth come praise and cursing. My brothers and sisters, this should not be. (James 3:10)

The concluding thought to James's teaching about taming the tongue gives an example of individuals whose words are both positive and negative, depending on the situation. Sometimes they praise God, and other times they curse people. This would be like mixing hot and cold water. The result is lukewarm, which has no value (consider Revelation 3:16).

It's like getting fresh water and salt water from the same source. It can't happen. Nor can a fruit tree produce two different types of fruit, both of which are contrary to its nature.

Some people alter their speech based on the circumstances. At church their words ooze with piety. Away from church—be it at home, during work, or around friends—they spew obscenities. This reveals their double-mindedness, vacillating between good and evil.

Where do our words fit on the spectrum of praising and cursing? How consistent is our speech in every area of our lives?

[Discover more about being double-minded in Psalm 119:113, James 1:8, and James 4:8.]

DAY 19: LIVE A GOOD LIFE
JAMES 3:13–16

Who is wise and understanding among you? Let them show it by their good life, by deeds done in the humility that comes from wisdom. (James 3:13)

James tells his audience to live a good life. But don't assume you know what this means. It isn't permission to live a life of ease or opulence or laziness. It's a call to pursue a God-honoring lifestyle. The wise person does this. By implication, the foolish person does not.

Living this good life isn't for ourselves or our benefit, at least not directly. It serves as an example to others. That means we live our good life as a witness, to serve as an encouragement to those around us.

This good life that James writes about refers to our actions, the deeds we do. To be of value, we must do these deeds in humility. And humility comes from godly wisdom (see "Day 2: Ask God for Wisdom").

The opposite of godly wisdom is worldly wisdom.

If we act with the wrong motives, this reflects man's wisdom and not God's. If our hearts harbor envy (that is, coveting what others have) or selfish ambition (that is, a greed for more), we're following the wisdom of the world. It's earthly, unspiritual, and demonic.

We shouldn't boast about our greedy plans (consider James 3:5). Doing so reveals the shallowness of our hearts, in the process causing others to envy what we have and what we will have. This encourages them to go down the same wrong path too.

Another warning of James is for those who deny their envious or ambitious hearts. Claiming that it's not true doesn't hide the reality of what is (1 John 1:10).

In this earthly wisdom, the kind that produces envy and selfish ambition, we find disorder and evil practices of every kind. This suggests that greed and envy are just the beginning. It's an out-of-control spiral, leading to even more behavior contrary to God's way and the call for us to lead a good life.

When we live a good life in honor of God, there's no place for greed or coveting.

Do we follow God's wisdom or the world's? When we get caught up in greed and coveting, how can we realign ourselves with God's way of living?

[Discover more about greed in Proverbs 15:27, Proverbs 28:25, Luke 12:15, and Ephesians 5:5. Read about coveting in Exodus 20:17, Deuteronomy 7:25, Micah 2:2, and Romans 13:9.]

DAY 20: WISDOM FROM ABOVE
JAMES 3:17–18

Wisdom that comes from heaven is first of all pure; then peace-loving, considerate, submissive, full of mercy and good fruit, impartial and sincere. (James 3:17)

In reading James's call for us to live a good life as aligned with godly wisdom, he talks a lot about earthly wisdom, but so far, he hasn't described godly wisdom. Now he does. He lists its qualities. We'll do well to follow them.

Godly wisdom starts with purity. Seven more attributes follow it: peace-loving, considerate, submissive, merciful, fruitful, impartial, and sincere.

Pure

Purity is living a moral lifestyle with chaste behavior. Purity is the opposite of sexual immorality, which Scripture frequently warns us against. Paul tells Timothy to treat women with absolute purity (1 Timothy 5:1–2). All men should have the same attitude toward all women. Likewise, Peter tells wives to live pure lives (1 Peter 3:1–2). We can extend this as wise advice to all women.

Peace-loving

Peace is a calmness, a lack of hostility. Paul tells the church in Thessalonica to live in peace with each other (1 Thessalonians 5:13). But more so than living in peace or pursuing peace, we should be peace-loving. We should delight in peace.

Considerate

To be considerate shows regard for people's needs and feelings. Being considerate is one quality Paul wants Titus to teach to others (Titus 3:1–2). One way to be considerate of others in humility is to value them above us (Philippians 2:3).

Submissive

When we're submissive, we're willing to yield to the authority of another. We are to submit to those in power (Romans 13:5). We're to submit to one another (Ephesians 5:21). And above all, we're to submit to God (Job 22:21).

Merciful

Being merciful is showing compassion. We should be merciful to others, just as God is merciful to us (Deuteronomy 4:31). In addition, Jesus teaches that the merciful will receive mercy (Matthew 5:7).

Fruitful

The idea of producing good fruit leads to positive outcomes in all that we do. Jesus talks about the need for us to be fruitful. Good trees—just like good people—produce good fruit (Matthew 7:17). Later he says that trees—and implicitly people—that don't produce good fruit will be cut down and burned (Luke 3:9).

Impartial

To be impartial is to avoid bias or prejudice, to not favor one person over another. It's being fair and just. We read throughout the Bible that God is just and fair (such as in 2 Thessalonians 1:6 and 1 John 1:9). And Jesus himself is just (John 5:30). So, too, should we be just (Leviticus 19:15 and Proverbs 31:9). We can also follow the instruction given to masters to do what is right and be fair (Colossians 4:1).

Sincere

Sincere means to be genuine, free from duplicity. We should do all things with sincerity. The New Testament writers talk about sincere love (1 Peter 1:22), sincere faith (1 Timothy 1:5), and a sincere heart (Hebrews 10:22). May these guide us to greater sincerity.

We should pursue wisdom from above, which is pure, peace-loving, considerate, submissive, merciful, fruitful, impartial, and sincere.

Which of these traits do we need to work on the most? How can we encourage others to pursue God's wisdom?

[Discover more godly characteristics in Galatians 5:22–23.]

DAY 21: FIGHTS AND QUARRELS
JAMES 4:1–3

What causes fights and quarrels among you? (James 4:1)

James opens this passage with a straightforward question that most people can identify with. He asks, "What causes you to fight and quarrel?" Since James addresses his letter to Jewish followers of Jesus, he's not talking about fighting with the world. He's talking about fighting with our own brothers and sisters in Christ.

If we've ever experienced conflict with another person, if we've fought and quarreled, we surely want to know the answer to this question. We hope

James will give us the solution to avoid these unpleasant interactions.

James does, but it may not be the answer we want. He asks, somewhat rhetorically, "Don't your conflicts come from your own desires?" He talks about a battle inside us, a battle in our minds. It's a struggle over what we desire.

The root is envy. We want what we don't have. We desire what someone else has. So, we kill to get it.

In extreme cases, this murdering of another to get what we want may be literal. Some people kill to get what they want, but most of us have never killed another person, nor would we even entertain the idea.

Most times, however, this image of committing murder is figurative. Jesus talks about murder and what it means. We know that the Ten Commandments prohibits murder, but Jesus expands on what this entails. Anyone who is angry at another, he says, is no less guilty (Matthew 5:21–22).

Implicitly, James says anger is a source of our infighting and bickering. Then he adds coveting to the list. We can't get what we want, so we argue and fight.

James & Jude Bible Study

Then James has the audacity to connect our fighting and quarreling with our prayer practices. He says we lack what we need because we don't ask God for it. But even when we ask, we don't get what we expect. The reason we don't receive answers to our prayers is because we have the wrong motivation. When wrong motives fuel our prayers, disappointment will surely result.

What is an example of praying with wrong motives? It's when our prayers are self-centered, asking for what will feed our pleasures.

Therefore, if we struggle in conflict—fighting and quarreling—with our brothers and sisters in Jesus, we must look at ourselves.

Do we want what others have? This is covetousness. Do we pray with wrong motives? This is selfishness. Correcting these two sins in ourselves should lessen our quarreling and our fighting.

How much do we struggle with anger and envy? How often do we pray with wrong motives?

[Discover more about envy in 1 Corinthians 13:4, Galatians 5:26, and 1 Peter 2:1. Read more about prayer in Mark 11:23–25, Philippians 4:6, and 1 John 5:14–15.]

DAY 22: SPIRITUAL ADULTERY
JAMES 4:4–6

You adulterous people, don't you know that friendship with the world means enmity against God? (James 4:4)

When we think of adultery, we think of an affair between two people who disregard their marriage vows of fidelity to their spouses and are unfaithful. They willfully turn away from the one they pledged themselves to in pursuit of another who seems more attractive or holds a greater appeal.

Yet we can also commit spiritual adultery.

Spiritual adultery occurs when we're unfaithful to God and the pledge we made to follow Jesus. We cheat on him, but not with our bodies. It's with our hearts. Our soul becomes unfaithful, and our actions follow it.

The Old Testament prophets talk about this spiritual idolatry. Jeremiah, Ezekiel, and Hosea all mention it specifically. The people are unfaithful to God. They turn to other gods, to idols, and to unholy pursuits. In doing so, they commit adultery against God.

Hosea addresses this unfaithfulness most profoundly. At God's direction, he marries a prostitute. She later runs away and cheats on him. But God tells his prophet to pursue her and redeem her. Hosea does just that. Then he uses his marital troubles as a scathing sermon illustration for God's people and their spiritual unfaithfulness.

Just as Hosea's wife cheated on him, so too have God's people cheated on him. Just as Hosea pursues and redeems his wife, God will pursue and redeem his people (Hosea 3:1–5). It's a beautiful illustration of unmerited love and restoration.

To help us better understand this in more practical terms, James expands on this idea of spiritual adultery. He says that if we align with the world, we oppose God. If we become friends with the world, we become an enemy of God.

Jesus says no man can serve two masters. We

can't love them both. We must choose. The result is loving one and hating the other, being devoted to the first and despising the second. These two masters standing in conflict with one another are God and money (Luke 16:13). If money served as a distraction two thousand years ago, how much more so today in our materialistic society?

Though the context of Jesus's teaching is serving God versus serving money, it's not wrong to consider money as exemplifying all that the world offers. Just as we can't serve both God and money, we can't align with our Father in heaven while embracing worldly perspectives that oppose him.

In the same way, James says we can't maintain our relationship with God if our focus is on the world and what it does.

To what extent have we pursued friendship with the world? When people look at our lifestyle, do they see us aligned with God or living like everyone else?

[Discover more about spiritual adultery in Jeremiah 3:6–18 and Ezekiel 23:1–49.]

BONUS CONTENT: JAMES IN THE OLD TESTAMENT

But he gives us more grace. That is why Scripture says: "God opposes the proud but shows favor to the humble." (James 4:6)

In his letter, James cites the Old Testament several times, mostly from the law of Moses. Here are the passages he references:

- James 2:8 quotes Leviticus 19:18
- James 2:11 quotes Exodus 20:14 and Deuteronomy 5:18, as well as Exodus 20:13 and Deuteronomy 5:17
- James 2:23 quotes Genesis 15:6
- James 4:4 alludes to Hosea 3:1

- James 4:6 quotes Proverbs 3:34

How well do we do at thanking God for his grace? What should we do to be less proud and more humble?

[Discover more about God's word in Psalm 119:11.]

DAY 23: SUBMIT TO GOD
JAMES 4:7–10

Submit yourselves, then, to God. Resist the devil, and he will flee from you. (James 4:7)

Next James writes to "Submit yourselves, then, to God." Why does he say *then*? It's because the idea of submitting to God follows from his prior discussion about loving God and not the world.

The best prescription to avoid committing spiritual idolatry, then, is to submit to God.

Following this instruction to submit to God comes part two of the prescription. It's to resist the devil. When we resist the enemy's temptations—in this case, to love what the world offers—he will stop harassing us. He will leave us alone. In fact, he will run away.

This idea of resisting the devil and the promise that he will flee from us is in the context of us not becoming friends with the world. We're not wrong, however, to extend this instruction and claim this promise in all areas of temptation.

We can best do this by coming near to God. This makes sense. As we draw toward God, we move away from the devil, from temptation. But this doesn't mean we eliminate the temptation, merely that we lessen it. And as we move closer to God, he moves closer to us.

Yet after this encouraging command, James slips into an increasingly confusing part of the passage. He tells us sinners to wash our hands and us double-minded people to purify our hearts.

Through Jesus's sacrificial death for our mistakes, he forgives our sins. But this doesn't remove our sin nature. Figuratively, we need to wash our hands of our sins, including trying to love the world. In like manner, as double-minded people —those trying to serve both God and the world— we must purify our hearts.

To highlight this point, James tells us to grieve, to mourn, and to wail. Instead of laughing, we should lament. Instead of having joy, we should have gloom.

These are not general commands to follow. Instead, this is James's instruction in response to our tendency to love the world and all that it offers, which pulls us away from God. Therefore, we must grieve, mourn, and wail.

He wraps up with a call to humility. We should humble ourselves before our Lord. When we do, he will lift us up.

Therefore, to deal with the pull of the world, we should submit to God, resist the devil, and humble ourselves in God's presence.

How well do we do at submitting to God and resisting the devil? In what ways are we double-minded?

[Discover more about submitting to God in Job 22:21 and Proverbs 3:6. Read about humility in Luke 14:11, Ephesians 4:2, and 1 Peter 5:5–6.]

DAY 24: WATCH WHAT WE SAY
JAMES 4:11–12

Brothers and sisters, do not slander one another. (James 4:11)

James tells us not to slander one another. To slander someone is to say something bad about them that damages their reputation. It's making a false statement with ill intent. It's even more distressing when we slander other followers of Jesus.

Slander is lying.

The Old Testament instructs us not to lie (Leviticus 19:11). We also shouldn't spread false reports or be a malicious witness (Exodus 23:1), which is to say we should not slander.

But it's more than just slander. James expands on the concept. He tells us to not speak against our brother or sister. This is a higher standard than not slandering one another. Spinning lies about someone else is certainly speaking against them. It sounds a lot like gossip.

It's possible, however, to state truth and still speak against someone. We must not do that either. Regardless if it's the truth or a lie, we shouldn't speak against other believers. The church will do well to embrace this truth that James proclaims.

Speaking against someone judges them. Judging others is God's domain and not ours. But when warning us not to judge others, James tells us to not judge our *neighbors*. This goes beyond our spiritual community that includes our brothers and sisters.

Recall Jesus's parable of the good Samaritan, which he uses to define the meaning of the word *neighbor* (Luke 10:25–37). In this story Jesus gives an example to consider: Thieves attack, beat, and rob a man walking on the road. A priest comes along but ignores the injured man. Next is a Levite, who likewise decides to not get involved. The third traveler is a Samaritan—a race the Jewish people despise. He helps the man and attends to his needs. The

Samaritan is the hero of this story and our example of who is our neighbor.

Adding to this trio of instructions—do not slander our brothers and sisters, do not speak against them, and do not judge our neighbors—James will later add the fourth consideration. In a few verses, he'll tell us to not grumble against each other (James 5:9).

To grumble is to mutter discontentment. It's to complain or be surly. Though we shouldn't grumble in any circumstance, in this case, James means specifically to not grumble about other followers of Jesus.

In all this, we need to watch what we say. We should not slander, speak against someone else, judge our neighbors, or grumble.

If we all did this, our world would be a much better place.

Which of these areas do we need to give more attention to? How can our example to watch what we say encourage others?

[Discover more about gossip in Proverbs 26:20, Romans 1:29–31, and 2 Corinthians 12:20.]

DAY 25: IF IT'S THE LORD'S WILL
JAMES 4:15–17

You ought to say, "If it is the Lord's will, we will live and do this or that." (James 4:15)

James rails against people who form grand plans to grow a business and make a lot of money. But this isn't a warning against planning or achieving success. It's a warning about depending on ourselves instead of God.

In doing so, we boast in our abilities, and we brag about what we'll accomplish. But we can't control what happens tomorrow. Only God can. We need to seek God first and not worry about the future (Matthew 6:33–34).

Instead, we should preface our plans with the stipulation that we'll do so if it's God's will. This is a wise perspective to have.

Consider the parable of the rich man with the abundant harvest. He didn't have space to store his crops, so he planned to tear down his barns and build bigger ones. Then he could live an easy life. But his plans mattered little because that night he died (Luke 12:16–21). Instead, he should have said, "If it's God's will I'll build bigger barns and store up for the future."

This may be why when Jesus taught his disciples how to pray, he told them to ask for their daily bread. He didn't say to ask for enough for the rest of the year, or for one month, or even for a week. Just what they needed to eat for one day (Matthew 6:9–13).

It's like when the Israelites were in the desert and needed food. God gave them manna. Each morning, they were to gather just what they needed for the day and no more. If they gathered too much, the excess spoiled. The only exception was on the day before the Sabbath when they needed to collect two days' worth. Then they could rest on the seventh day (Exodus 16:13–30).

Again, this isn't an excuse to not plan. It's a

James & Jude Bible Study

lesson to not brag about our plans, which we should yield to God's will. Paul had specific plans of where he should tell others about Jesus. But the Holy Spirit gave him a different direction, and Paul obeyed (Acts 16:6–10).

Paul held his plans loosely, according to how God led him. We, too, should hold our plans loosely. God has the last word (Proverbs 16:1).

The point of this passage is that God is in control. We are not. Our plans should reflect this reality.

How do we do at yielding our plans to God's will? When have we failed to plan and suffered as a result?

[Discover more about planning in Proverbs 6:6 and Luke 14:28–33.]

DAY 26: WEEP AND WAIL
JAMES 5:1–6

Now listen, you rich people, weep and wail because of the misery that is coming on you. (James 5:1)

James moves from talking about people who brag and boast about their plans of making a lot of money to addressing rich people. There's a connection, with the first concern producing the second. He tells these rich people to weep and wail over what will soon befall them. They won't be able to hold on to their wealth. They will die, and their money will mean nothing.

Consider Jesus's parable about the rich man and the poor beggar, Lazarus. The rich man lives a life of ease, while Lazarus suffers. Then they both die.

Lazarus receives comfort from Father Abraham, while the rich man receives torment in hell (Luke 16:19–31).

The rich man didn't recognize his eternal fate until it was too late. Though enjoying wealth in this life, he receives misery in the next. This, most assuredly, is a reason to weep and wail.

This isn't the outcome of all rich people, however, but only those who gain wealth the wrong way. Consider James's four descriptions of what to avoid.

First, they hoarded wealth. Instead, they should have used their blessings to bless others (see Genesis 12:2–3 and Proverbs 11:25). Accumulating for ourselves is selfish and wrong. This doesn't mean we shouldn't save for the future, but we should do so as good stewards with the mindset of generosity.

Next, they gained wealth by cheating their workers out of the pay they earned. Jacob charged his father-in-law, Laban, with this, claiming Laban changed his wages ten times (Genesis 31:41). Note that God prospered Jacob anyway.

Third, they lived in luxury and sought pleasure. They were self-centered with their wealth. They held on to their money tightly, with selfish intent. This is a common outcome of people who hoard wealth, which they gain at the expense of their workers (Deuteronomy 24:14).

Last, they condemned and murdered the innocent one, despite him posing no threat (James 5:6). We can see this as a reference to Jesus, with those who took part in his death being guilty of rejecting him (Mark 14:62–64). Many versions of the Bible take a broader view in their rendering of *the innocent one*, applying it to all righteous people or everyone who is innocent. These rich people do so without justification. Their wealth comes at the expense of these people.

These four scenarios will position wealthy people to need to weep and mourn over the misery that will soon befall them.

May we avoid their errors. With God's help, we can.

What should our perspective be toward money and wealth? What must we do to avoid the errors James identifies with these rich people?

[Discover more about wealth in Luke 16:10–12, 1 Timothy 6:17, and Revelation 3:17.]

DAY 27: BE PATIENT
JAMES 5:7–11

Be patient, then, brothers and sisters, until the Lord's coming.
(James 5:7)

James tells us to be patient. It's imperative. It's a trait we must adopt. But for how long should we be patient? Until Jesus comes again. That means we need to be patient for the rest of our time here on earth, likely until we die. That's a long time. It means that through our whole life, we must remain patient.

He then gives us some examples of patience.

First, consider a farmer. He doesn't plant one day and harvest the next. He waits for his seeds to germinate and grow, for rain to fall on them so they can produce a good crop. In the same way, we must patiently wait for Jesus to return.

Next, James addresses complaining. Since the preceding verses and the following verses talk about patience, complaining must have something to do with it. In truth, when we complain about someone or something, it reflects an impatience. Yet to hold our tongue and remain quiet when we want to speak reveals our patience.

Third, he reminds us of the prophets and their steadfast endurance as they proclaimed God's messages to people who mostly didn't want to hear it and weren't responsive. Most of God's prophets toiled for years with little apparent success. Of course, we know people responded to the message Jonah proclaimed for just a few days, but he seems to be the exception. If only all the other prophets realized such success with their messages. Instead, they embraced patience as they did what God told them to do.

Last, James reminds us of the endurance of Job. Satan robbed him of everything. He stripped Job of his possessions, his children, and even his health. As Job clung to life, all he had left was a critical wife and four unhelpful friends.

Yet Job persevered through his travail. As a

reward, God restored his health, doubled his possessions, and gave him ten more children. But if Job had been impatient, he never would have gotten to that point or realized the outcome God had planned for him. May we have the patient endurance of Job.

We can receive all these as examples to encourage us to be patient in all we do throughout our lives, but the primary teaching is to be patient until Jesus returns. May he find us ready when he does.

Which of these examples of patience do you most identify with? How patient are we as we wait for Jesus's return?

[Discover more about Jesus's return in Matthew 24:42–44, Mark 13:32–37, and Luke 12:35–48.]

BONUS CONTENT: DO NOT SWEAR

Above all, my brothers and sisters, do not swear—not by heaven or by earth or by anything else. All you need to say is a simple "Yes" or "No." (James 5:12)

Next, James tells us not to swear. Since this doesn't seem to tie in with the verses that precede it or the verses that follow it, we can view this as a stand-alone teaching.

We shouldn't swear by heaven, by earth, or by anything else. Instead, we should simply say "Yes" or "No." Our word should be enough. We don't need to swear by a higher authority or a greater power.

In fact, we shouldn't swear by anything else. If

we do, we'll receive condemnation. This suggests that swearing by anything beyond ourselves is a sin. Don't do it.

Let our *yes* be yes and our *no* be no. May we then live with integrity to prove the reliability of what we say.

When we tell someone "Yes" or "No," how likely are they to believe us? What does it say about us if we feel we need to swear by someone or something else?

[Discover more about swearing in Leviticus 19:12 and Matthew 5:33–37.]

DAY 28: PRAY
JAMES 5:13–16

Confess your sins to each other and pray for each other so that you may be healed. (James 5:16)

Next, James talks about prayer. He packs a lot of insight into this short four-verse passage. He addresses four items to encourage us to pray.

First, if we're in trouble, we should pray. Trouble means a state of distress or discomfort. Given this definition, we all face trouble at some point. Though we may want to react in anger or treat it as inevitable, the biblical response is to pray.

Next, if we're happy, we should sing songs of praise. On a quick read, this seems to contradict

James 4:9, which says to grieve, mourn, and wail. But as we covered in "Day 26: Weep and Wail," this is the response for those living in sin or who are double-minded, not for those who are genuinely happy.

To be happy means to be cheerful, have joy, or experience satisfaction. With this understanding, we're all happy at some point. The response is to sing praises, which is a form of prayer. And for those—like me—who can't carry a tune, we can go directly to praising God in prayer.

Third, if we're sick, we should seek prayer from our elders. Since sickness is a form of trouble, we've already prayed about it ourselves. Now it's time to get others involved.

If we are the one who prays for someone's healing, we should anoint them with oil in Jesus's name. Though some interpret *anointing* to suggest taking tangible steps to alleviate the sickness, it seems more consistent with the biblical narrative to view this as a symbolic gesture. Even so, if we can help physically address their sickness, we should. In doing so, we do what we can to help and trust God with the rest.

When these healing prayers come from a place of faith, God will restore them to health. Though we may struggle with the implications of what it means when God doesn't heal, we should remember that God is sovereign, and we are not. Maybe our faith wasn't as strong as needed, or we were insincere. Perhaps God had a greater purpose in not answering our request the way we wanted. Regardless, this apparent failure should not shake our confidence in God but instead cause us to stand in awe of his omniscience—his all-knowing power.

If their illness stems from a sin, they'll receive forgiveness. This is perplexing because Jesus has already forgiven them their sins: past, present, and future. Might this refer to the need to address unconfessed sins or deliberate sins they persist in committing? Regardless, this moves us into the final prayer consideration.

Fourth, we are to, therefore, confess our sins to each other and pray for each other so that we may receive healing. This command couples confession with restoration.

We're then encouraged with the truth that when righteous people pray, it's powerful and accomplishes much.

May this exemplify our prayers.

Which of these four items about prayer do we need to give more attention to? How do we react when we don't see the answers to prayer that we expect?

[Discover more about prayer in Matthew 6:5, Matthew 21:22, Acts 1:14, Romans 12:12, and Ephesians 6:18.]

DAY 29: ELIJAH'S EXAMPLE
JAMES 5:17–18

Elijah was a human being, even as we are. He prayed earnestly that it would not rain, and it did not rain on the land for three and a half years. (James 5:17)

We read about Elijah in the Old Testament, primarily in 1 Kings 17 to 2 Kings 2.

Elijah is a prophet of God. His ministry mostly occurs during the reign of Israel's King Ahab. Ahab is an evil king who—along with his equally evil wife, Jezebel—opposes God and those who serve him.

Our first encounter with Elijah is when he approaches Ahab with a bold statement. The prophet informs the king that there will be a years-long drought. There will be no dew or rain until Elijah says so (1 Kings 17–18).

What a way to start a ministry.

Because the drought also affects Elijah, God sends him to the Kerith Ravine. There he drinks from the brook, and ravens bring him food. But eventually the brook dries up.

Then God sends Elijah to a widow in Zarephath. Though she has limited food, God multiplies it so she can feed Elijah, her son, and herself for the rest of the drought.

After three years of no rain, God sends Elijah to appear again before King Ahab. What follows is a showdown on Mount Carmel between Elijah and the prophets of Baal. They each prepare an altar and a sacrifice but don't light the fire. The prophets of Baal call on him to send forth fire, but nothing happens.

With them having failed, Elijah drenches his altar with water. He calls on the Lord. God sends down fire, which burns the sacrifice, the wood, the stones, the soil, and even the water.

In this, God dramatically shows his power, while proving that Baal has none. Elijah orders the execution of the prophets of Baal. He then tells Ahab that rain is coming. While Ahab eats his dinner, Elijah goes to the top of the mountain to pray for rain.

Elijah prays, but nothing happens. He prays again, still nothing. After he prays the seventh time, his servant sees a small cloud forming in the distance. The sky grows black, the winds pick up, and a heavy rain falls.

This is the story of Elijah that James refers to.

Elijah is a person, just like us. He prays for a drought, and it doesn't rain. Later, when he prays for rain, there is a downpour.

If he is like us, what can we learn from him to inform our prayers?

First, he didn't just pray. He prayed in earnest. It's purposeful, sincere, and serious.

Next, he didn't pray just one time, but seven times. In this, we see he prayed until he received his answer.

May we do the same.

How earnest are our prayers? How many times do we pray before we give up?

[Discover more about praying in faith in Matthew 21:22 and Mark 11:22–25.]

DAY 30: BRING THEM BACK
JAMES 5:19–20

Whoever turns a sinner from the error of their way will save them from death and cover over a multitude of sins. (James 5:20)

Taken in isolation, this verse seems straightforward. It's about sharing the good news of Jesus so that people repent —that is, they stop doing what they're doing and pursue a different path to follow Jesus. Through Jesus, they will not experience eternal death but will instead experience eternal life with him. His death on the cross will cover their sins, a multitude of them.

Yet this verse isn't a call to add converts to the

kingdom of God. This verse is about those who already follow Jesus.

Read the verse that precedes this one. It gives needed clarity.

James addresses "my brothers and sisters." This means they're already followers of Jesus. James writes about the possibility of one of them wandering from the truth, the truth of who Jesus is and what he did to save us.

This wandering could be anything from a short-term distraction all the way to intentionally abandoning their faith. Regardless, it seems they've walked away from Jesus.

Should we just let them go? Of course not! Someone needs to bring them back.

The person who restores them into a relationship with Jesus and his Father will save them from death and cover a multitude of sins. We could debate if this means they have backslidden or if they've lost their salvation and need to repent anew, but that distracts us from two key points in this passage.

First, we need to guard our own faith and faith practices. We must make sure we don't wander from the truth.

This can occur when we profess to following

Jesus but live like the rest of the world. It can also happen when we take elements of biblical faith and add to them spiritual practices of other religions that, at their core, are contrary to Jesus and what he teaches.

Other situations that might cause us to wander from the truth are anything that produces a crisis that confronts our faith. Though we can't ensure these things won't happen, we can take precautions to minimize the chances of it occurring. We can also ask God to help us remain focused on him.

Second, we need to be ready to be the second person in this passage, the one who brings the wandering soul back to Jesus. Though the focus of many is on converts, far fewer are interested in growing disciples, which, incidentally, is what Jesus tells us to do (Matthew 28:19–20). Even fewer people give attention to those who wander off.

While James promises no tangible reward for those of us who restore someone who wanders, we can know we've done our part to keep them from death and cover their sins.

What steps can we take to make sure we don't wander from

the truth of Jesus? Who has wandered away that we can help?

[Discover more about restoration in Galatians 6:1.]

THE LETTER OF JUDE
JUDE 1:1–2

Jude, a servant of Jesus Christ and a brother of James, To those who have been called, who are loved in God the Father and kept for Jesus Christ. (Jude 1:1)

Jude writes his letter to all who have been called by God, loved by the Father, and kept by Jesus.

This all-encompassing audience embraces all Christians everywhere, including us today.

Let's dig into this rich but often-overlooked book.

DAY 31: CONTEND FOR THE FAITH
JUDE 1:3–4

I felt compelled to write and urge you to contend for the faith that was once for all entrusted to God's holy people. (Jude 1:3)

Jude opens his letter with an explanation of what he wants to accomplish. Though his intention was to write about our common salvation, which he was eager to do, he changed his mind.

Instead, he feels compelled to address a different topic. He doesn't explain about this compulsion, but it's easy to perceive it as coming from the Holy Spirit's direction. What is this new topic? It's that we contend for the faith. We must endeavor to hold on to what God entrusted to us.

In contending for the faith, we strive among opposition and against difficulties. We struggle. It's like running a race that we strain to win, desiring to cross the finish line first and win our prize.

Though we might assume this struggle is against the world, it is not. It comes from within, from among followers of Jesus. Though masquerading as believers in the Messiah, they are, in fact, ungodly people. Just as certain individuals slipped into Jesus's church two thousand years ago, the same occurs today.

It should be easy to spot one ungodly person among God's holy flock, but Jude gives us two specific traits to look for.

First, they distort God's grace into a freedom to sin. More specifically, they think that Jesus's complete forgiveness grants them a license for immorality. God's grace—which gives us good things we don't deserve—is freely offered. We do not and cannot earn it. But we certainly shouldn't abuse it and assume we can live however we want, without ramifications.

Paul addresses this issue of abusing God's grace in his letter to the church in Rome. He asks rhetorically if we should persist in sin to better showcase God's grace. In case we don't know the answer, he gives it to us. "Absolutely not!" Through Jesus we have died to sin. Therefore, we should no longer live in it (Romans 6:1–2).

As Jesus's followers, sin should no longer be our master. He freed us from an impossible-to-follow law and gave us his grace instead. Therefore, we shouldn't be slaves to sin. Instead, we should pursue righteousness, that is, we should live rightly (Romans 6:11–16).

There's a second thing these ungodly people, who have infiltrated our gatherings, do. They deny Jesus's sovereignty and lordship. John also addresses this in his letter to the early believers (1 John 2:21–23). Jesus is our Lord. He died on the cross to save us, sacrificing himself to redress our sins and make us right with Father God.

If Jesus isn't who he says he is, we're foolish to follow him. Yet if Jesus is everything he claims to be, we're foolish not to.

May we guard against ungodly people who want to abuse God's grace and diminish Jesus.

When have we overrelied on God's grace? What must we do to contend for the faith and finish our race strong?

[Discover more about running our race in 1 Corinthians 9:24, Galatians 2:2, Galatians 5:7, and Hebrews 12:1.]

DAY 32: GRACE AND JUDGMENT
JUDE 1:5–7

Though you already know all this, I want to remind you that the Lord at one time delivered his people out of Egypt, but later destroyed those who did not believe. (Jude 1:5)

Jude often writes in triplets to illustrate his points. I appreciate the rhythm of this form and the trio of examples he gives to aid us in understanding. Such is the case with today's passage.

Jude reminds his audience of what they already know. Yet he feels the need to tell them again, lest they forget this important lesson. He's building on his teaching about those who misunderstand God's grace and think that what they do doesn't matter. He wants to make sure they know.

He gives us three examples to show God's judgment. If one doesn't click with us, hopefully another will.

First, he reminds them of the people who fled Egypt. God rescued them, but their repeated unacceptable behavior while in the desert results in them not placing their trust in him or believing in his promises. As a result, all those people twenty years of age and older die in the desert. This even includes Moses. It's their descendants who move to take the land God promised for them (Numbers 14:29). Only Joshua and Caleb escape this punishment.

Second, Jude calls our attention to the angels who rebelled against God. They are bound and imprisoned until the day of judgment. We get a sense of these fallen angels when the "sons of God" —which we understand to be rebellious angels— marry human women and produce offspring (Genesis 6:1–4).

In a parallel passage, Peter also talks about these sinful angels chained in darkness awaiting their final judgment (2 Peter 2:4–10). Jude, however, likely alludes to a nonbiblical text—such as the Book of Enoch—that his audience knows well, even if we don't.

Third, we read about Sodom and Gomorrah, towns which are also mentioned in Peter's passage. They receive punishment for their sins. We typically understand this as their sexual perversion and immoral lifestyle, which Jude concurs with. Yet Ezekiel writes that Sodom's sin is a failure to help the poor (Ezekiel 16:49). Either way, they receive judgment for their grievous mistakes (Genesis 19:23–29).

All three reminders point to God's judgment, which results from sin. The first example, however, addresses the sins of God's chosen people. They, too, receive the punishment their sins deserve.

Though we know that through Jesus we won't receive punishment as his followers, we must take care lest we fall away.

Which of these three examples do we most resonate with? How should we balance the grace God gives us with the possibility of punishment?

[Discover more about God's judgment in Matthew 12:36 and John 5:24. Read about the assurance of salvation in John 3:16 and Romans 8:1.]

DAY 33: SLANDER
JUDE 1:8–10

These people slander whatever they do not understand. (Jude 1:10)

Jude continues his warning about these godless people who slipped into their gatherings. He calls them dreamers. While this could be an actual dream, even a vision, their dreams could be figurative. It might refer to what they want to happen, building on the illusion —their dream—that they can persist in living a sinful life and won't face judgment for their willful disobedience.

These ungodly people do three things.

First, they pollute their own bodies. This pollution comes from their willful engagement in sinful behavior, from doing what they know is wrong and thinking it's okay because God's grace covers their disobedience. Their bodies will suffer from their delusion.

Next, they reject authority. This could be the authority of their spiritual leaders here on earth. Or it could be God's authority. Either way, they don't want to be accountable for what they do. Instead, they persist in their sins.

Third, they slander angels. This item is challenging to grasp. Though Jude gives us an example, it's still hard to discern how to apply it. It comes from a non-biblical source that his audience would have known well. It's a story about the archangel Michael arguing with the devil about the body of Moses, perhaps referring to Deuteronomy 34:6. In doing so, Michael doesn't accuse the devil of slander. He simply says, "The Lord rebuke you."

This may be a good principle to follow when debating with another believer about a matter of faith. Instead of speaking ill about them—that is, slandering them—we should turn the situation over to God and let him handle it according to his all-knowing power.

Yet these ungodly people slander what they do not understand.

This gives me pause. Too often I've heard ministers ridicule ideas and people they didn't understand. This might come from ignorance or an unwillingness to try. Though I won't label them as ungodly, aligning with the context of Jude's writing, I do worry about them leading people astray.

Whether we're a leader or not, we must guard our words, taking care to watch what we say so that we don't slander others.

We should worry about what we say, and let God deal with what others say.

How well do we do at respecting the authorities in our lives? What should we do to make sure we don't slander others?

[Discover more about slander in Leviticus 19:16, 1 Corinthians 4:12–13, and James 4:11.]

DAY 34: WOE TO THEM
JUDE 1:11

Woe to them! They have taken the way of Cain; they have rushed for profit into Balaam's error; they have been destroyed in Korah's rebellion. (Jude 1:11)

In today's passage, Jude compares ungodly men *in* the church to Cain, Balaam, and Korah. Each of these men has a connection with God, as do ungodly men in the church. Despite this, however, we best know them for their failings.

Cain

Two brothers each give God an offering. God does not accept Cain's, but he does accept Abel's. Cain is angry. Knowing Cain's thoughts, God urges caution. He tells Cain to rule over his sinful ideas, the temptation to do wrong. But Cain doesn't listen.

In a jealous rage, Cain kills Abel and becomes the world's first murderer (Genesis 4:3–8).

When Jude says we need to avoid the way of Cain, he means we must control our thoughts and desires to do wrong. We must heed his warning.

The way of Cain is failing to control the temptation to sin (1 John 3:12).

Balaam

A quick read of Balaam's story in Numbers 22–24 shows a man who affirms God, hears God's voice, and obeys. God tells Balaam to not go, and he stays. Then God tells him to go, and he goes—but God's angry because he does.

The first time God says "no" should've been enough. But Balaam is greedy and asks again. It's like kids pestering their folks for something. It's irritating.

Besides greed, Balaam mixes his pursuit of God with divination, a practice the Bible forbids (Leviticus 19:26). Many do this today. They pick select parts of various religions or philosophies to form their own belief system. But a made-up religion accomplishes nothing of eternal value.

We must carefully guard against Balaam's error of greed and mixing religions.

Later, when Joshua leads the people to take the land God promised them, we read that Balaam is among the casualties (Joshua 13:22).

Korah

Korah comes from the tribe of Levi. God assigns the Levites various temple-related tasks. They are not, however, to serve as priests. This falls only to Aaron and his descendants.

But Korah doesn't like this. He advocates that all people are holy, have God in them, and should be elevated to the level of priests. Although Jesus will later usher in these changes, God had a different plan for his people then, which Moses supported, and Korah opposed.

Korah stirs up some followers, insisting on equal status for all. He and Moses have a showdown.

Moses wins and receives God's affirmation. Korah loses. The ground opens. He and his family fall in and die. Korah's rebellion ends with his death (Numbers 16:1–35).

Korah will forever be associated with a failed uprising against God and opposing God's appointed leader.

We must avoid the way of Cain, the greed of Balaam, and the rebellion of Korah. Woe to them, and to us if we follow their examples.

In what ways are we like Cain, Balaam, and Korah? How can we best guard against repeating their errors?

[Discover more about Cain in Hebrews 11:4. Read more about Balaam in 2 Peter 2:15 and Revelation 2:14.]

DAY 35: BLEMISHES
JUDE 1:12–13

These people are blemishes at your love feasts. (Jude 1:12)

Jude continues his discourse about ungodly people in the church. He says they're blemishes at our love feasts.

Though *love feasts* may strike us as an odd phrase, let's simply understand it as the times we gather in Jesus's name. This includes special celebrations or banquets. In an actual sense, we can think of our *love feasts* as partaking in Holy Communion.

During any of these times of community celebration, these ungodly people in our midst join in with no hesitation. In doing so, these shepherds feed only themselves, instead of caring for their flock, as a good shepherd should (Ezekiel 34:2–8). These ungodly people are selfish and self-centered.

In a departure from giving us three examples, this time Jude gives four. These metaphors can help us see the error of their ways.

Clouds Without Rain

These ungodly people in our gatherings are like clouds that don't produce rain (Proverbs 25:14). They have the appearance of potential, but they fail to deliver. They are worthless. Just as rain falls to the earth to nourish plants so they can grow, we expect the same from these people in a spiritual sense. But they give us nothing, despite their appearance.

Trees Without Fruit

In like manner, these ungodly people are like fruit trees that do not produce a harvest (Luke 3:8–9 and Luke 6:43–44). They have leaves but no fruit. They're not functioning as God intends them to behave.

These trees take up space and consume

resources but provide nothing to eat. What good are they? None.

Waves of Foam

Next, consider waves on the sea. They're wild, uncontrollable. They roil up foam and nothing more. So, too, are ungodly people in our midst. We must guard against them, lest their undertow pull us from safety and cause us to drown.

Wandering Stars

Last, consider stars up in the night sky. Though we now know they follow a prescribed path, they appear to wander in a black void of nothingness. This is their domain forever (2 Peter 2:17). This is the lot of ungodly people in our gatherings. May we be diligent to avoid their outcome.

The first two examples—clouds without rain and trees without fruit—give us the image of a promise that doesn't produce. The last two examples—waves of foam and wandering stars—provide images of futility.

We must avoid all four.

How might we have shown promise and failed to produce? What might we do that shows futility?

[Discover more about futility in Psalm 94:11 and Romans 1:21.]

DAY 36: JUDGE AND CONVICT THE UNGODLY
JUDE 1:14–16

These people are grumblers and faultfinders; they follow their own evil desires; they boast about themselves and flatter others for their own advantage. (Jude 1:16)

We read about Enoch in the book of Genesis. We know how long he lives, that he walks faithfully with God, and that God takes him away—skipping death to be with God (Genesis 5:21–24). But Scripture doesn't tell us anything Enoch says. Again, Jude quotes a non-biblical source.

In it, Enoch prophesies about God coming with his holy army to judge everyone and convict the ungodly. Given the theme of Jude's book, we should assume this refers to the ungodly people who claim to follow Jesus. These ungodly individuals will face conviction for the ungodly acts they committed and the defiant words they proclaim against God.

Three areas emerge as their primary errors.

Grumble and Find Fault

These ungodly people in our churches specialize in grumbling and finding fault. They criticize others. They're chronic complainers.

While not everyone who grumbles and finds fault is an ungodly person, it's certainly a trait we must avoid. And if this is an area we struggle with, we must seek God to help us work through it and put it in our past.

After Korah's rebellion, which we talked about in "Day 34: Woe to Them," the people grumble against Moses and Aaron. As a result, many die (Numbers 16:41 and 49). This may be what Paul has in mind when he tells the church in Corinth to not grumble (1 Corinthians 10:10).

Follow Evil Desires

Next, these ungodly people in Jesus's church follow their own evil desires. God will come to judge and convict them of their error. They don't do what is good. Instead, they do what is wrong, what is evil, as driven by their own selfish cravings. Recall the self-centered shepherds in "Day 35: Blemishes."

Boast and Flatter

The third primary area where these ungodly people sin is in boasting and flattering. They boast about themselves instead of the Lord. They brag about what they've done and what they plan to do (James 4:14–16). Instead, we should only boast in the Lord (2 Corinthians 10:17). Continuing in their unhealthy speech, they flatter others for their own personal gain (Romans 16:18).

Which of these three areas do we need to give the most attention to? How have we harmed Jesus's church through these ungodly practices?

[Discover more about flattery in Psalm 12:2–4, Proverbs 26:28, and 1 Thessalonians 2:5.]

BONUS CONTENT: UNGODLY

". . . to judge everyone, and to convict all of them of all the ungodly acts they have committed in their ungodliness, and of all the defiant words ungodly sinners have spoken against him." (Jude 1:15)

The theme of Jude's concise letter is ungodliness within the church. The word *ungodly* appears five times in this one-chapter book, representing four verses, along with the heading that was later added before verse 3.

If you want to explore these specific *ungodly* verses, here they are:

- Jude 1:4

- Jude 1:8
- Jude 1:15
- Jude 1:18

Most of the Bible's mentions of ungodly people refer to those in the world. But Jude focuses his writing on ungodly people within Jesus's church and who profess to follow him.

We will do well to avoid repeating their error.

What do we think about the idea of ungodly people within the church? How should we respond when we encounter people in our gatherings who exhibit these ungodly traits?

[Discover more about the ungodly in 1 Peter 4:18, 2 Peter 2:4–6, and 2 Peter 3:7.]

DAY 37: SCOFFERS
JUDE 1:17–19

"In the last times there will be scoffers who will follow their own ungodly desires." (Jude 1:18)

Jude now cites Jesus's disciples. They prophesied that in the future—the last days—we will see scoffers who follow their own ungodly desires. Jude may be referring to the writing of Peter, who addresses this topic twice in his second letter (2 Peter 2:1–3 and 2 Peter 3:3–4).

Paul also shares this sentiment (Acts 20:29–30, 2 Timothy 3:1–5, and 2 Timothy 4:3–4) and John alludes to it (2 John 1:7–11). Although we don't have any writings from the other apostles to confirm this, it's likely they share this concern too.

Jude gives us three characteristics of these immoral scoffers.

Cause Division

These ungodly scoffers cause division within Jesus's church. Remember that they aren't attacking it from the outside. They're causing dissension from within.

We may naturally expect opposition from the world and guard against it. What's more insidious—and damaging—is when divisiveness comes from within the church, from people who purport to follow Jesus.

Yet too often, we don't expect internal threats. We aren't looking out for them. As such, they creep in without us realizing it. And once their division takes root, it's hard to eradicate its hold.

Follow Natural Instincts

Next, these ungodly scoffers follow their own natural instincts. Though some natural instincts are positive, such as the sense to run from danger, this is not what Jude means. He's referring to sensual cravings and carnal pursuits.

These people are worldly minded and not God focused. Therefore, we shouldn't expect their behavior to align with what's in the best interest of Jesus and his church. Instead, we should expect the opposite. We need to guard against them because their focus will produce the wrong outcomes.

Do Not Have the Spirit

Last, these ungodly scoffers do not have God's Spirit. It may be they never received the Holy Spirit. But if they never received the Holy Spirit, that means they're not truly Jesus's followers. Jesus promised the Holy Spirit to all who believe in him (Luke 24:49, John 14:26, and Acts 1:4–5).

An alternative understanding, therefore, is that they do have the Holy Spirit living within them, but they stopped listening to him. They ignore him and have shut him out of their lives.

This means they're trying to live under their own power and not God's. As such, the Holy Spirit doesn't direct what they do.

Though we may all have times when we cause

division, are worldly minded, or don't listen to the Holy Spirit, these should be rare and not typical.

If these are common occurrences in our lives, however, we may be in danger of becoming the ungodly people Jude warns about. And it's a warning we should seriously consider.

What can we do to make sure we don't cause division among Jesus's followers? How can we become more open to hearing and obeying the Holy Spirit God sent to guide us?

[Discover more about divisions in Romans 16:17 and 1 Corinthians 1:10.]

DAY 38: PRAY IN THE SPIRIT
JUDE 1:20–21

Keep yourselves in God's love as you wait for the mercy of our Lord Jesus Christ to bring you to eternal life. (Jude 1:21)

So far, the text of Jude's letter has focused on the characteristics of ungodly people within the church. This helps us know how to identify their threats. It also tells us traits we need to guard against in our personal lives.

Jude now takes a positive turn and tells us what we should do. It stands as his prescription to live rightly for Jesus as we wait to join him in eternity. That means we should spend the rest of our lives perfecting how these actions manifest themselves in our lives.

Jude's three directives for us as Jesus's followers are:

Build Up Our Faith

We know that faith is important as we follow Jesus. We began our journey with him by faith (Romans 10:10). Now we want to grow in that faith. We want our faith to develop. This is easy to say but harder to do.

The word *faith* and its derivatives appear throughout Scripture, in over four hundred verses. Except for the ultra-short letter of 2 John, every New Testament book mentions faith in multiple verses. That's a lot of resources to teach us about faith.

The best-known verse about faith gives us a helpful definition. It says, "Faith is confidence in what we hope for and assurance about what we do not see" (Hebrews 11:1). The rest of that chapter reminds us of Old Testament characters who exhibited great faith. We will do well to follow their examples.

Pray in the Holy Spirit

In contrast, the Bible gives us few verses about praying in the Spirit. Paul does, however, tell the church in Ephesus to do just that (Ephesians 6:18). In general, we should rely on the Holy Spirit to inform our prayers. When we listen, he will reveal to us God's heart. We then align our prayers to what our Father in heaven wants, as guided by the Holy Spirit.

The Holy Spirit shows up most prominently in the early church, as seen in the book of Acts. We can learn from their example and let the Holy Spirit guide us in all things, including our prayers.

Keep in God's Love

Our last action is to stay in God's love. As we remain in his love, we will love him first and love others as much as ourselves. These stand as God's two greatest commandments (Matthew 22:37–40).

The Bible gives us over six hundred verses that mention love. Every book in the New Testament (except Acts) mentions love multiple times, with the book of John leading them all.

We find the best-known passage about love,

however, in 1 Corinthians 13. We strive to follow the characteristics of love that Paul details in this letter (1 Corinthians 13:4–7).

How can we better align our prayers with the Holy Spirit's leading? How well do we do at loving God more than anything else?

[Discover more about the Holy Spirit in Romans 14:17–18, Romans 15:13, 1 Corinthians 6:19, and Ephesians 4:30.]

DAY 39: HELP THOSE IN NEED
JUDE 1:22–23

Be merciful to those who doubt. (Jude 1:22)

Jude continues his prescription for the faithful. Building on the three instructions we covered in the prior chapter—"Day 38: Pray in the Spirit"—now we receive three more actions to take as Jesus's committed followers.

They are to help the doubters, save the sinners, and rescue the corrupt. We can rightly tie each one of these back to the theme of this book, which warns us to watch out for the ungodly who have infiltrated our faith communities.

Help Doubters

An element of doubt is normal for those who follow Jesus in faith. If the potential for doubt to creep in didn't exist, we wouldn't require faith. It would be a sure thing. Therefore, we shouldn't concern ourselves when an occasional sliver of doubt slips in. We should turn it over to God and trust him in all things.

Yet with some people doubt is more prevalent, threatening to torpedo their faith. The ungodly in their spiritual gatherings fuel their doubt. They cause these struggling people to question what they've been taught, their beliefs, and their practices.

It's up to us to draw them back to faith and their faith community. Jude writes that we're to show them mercy. In this passage, we can best think of mercy as to help them, to show them compassion. We need to undo what the ungodly did.

Save Sinners

Next, Jude writes that we are to save others. We do this by snatching them out of the fire. The reference to fire suggests perpetual punishment in the torment of hell, of eternal damnation. These people have not yet followed Jesus, and we need to point them to him as their Lord and Savior.

Again, considering the theme of ungodly people in the church, we get a sense that they are the ones who have kept these people from Jesus.

Rescue the Corrupt

The third action Jude charges us with is to rescue people corrupted by their sin practices. They are so enmeshed in evil that we should only approach them with much caution, lest we get sucked in as well. Jude uses the word *fear*. This is a God-honoring fear but not a paralyzing one. We must act, trusting God to protect us. Yet we must proceed with vigilance.

As with saving the sinners, we get the sense that the ungodly people in our churches may be the reason these individuals are corrupted by sin.

Who do we know that fits in one of these three categories? What should be our response?

[Discover more about these three areas in Matthew 28:17, Mark 2:17, and 1 Corinthians 15:33. Also see "Day 30: Bring them Back."]

DAY 40: PRAISE HIM
JUDE 1:24–25

To him who is able to keep you from stumbling and to present you before his glorious presence without fault and with great joy. (Jude 1:24)

In considering the ungodly people in our midst, Jude warns us to contend for our faith. Then he encourages us in how to respond. Now Jude ends his letter with praise to God.

His words of praise come to us in two parts, one phrase per verse.

The first passage praises God, who keeps us from stumbling in this life. He prepares us to come before him in glory in the next life—a supernatural one—to live with him forever. We arrive before him with a clean record, unblemished. Our sinless state is not a result of anything we have done. Instead, it's what Jesus did for us. Given this, we approach God with much joy.

When we encounter the Father, Son, and Holy Spirit in heaven after we die, we won't carry shame or bear guilt for all the mistakes we've made. Jesus took that all away from us in his ultimate sacrifice to end all sacrifices. His actions make us right with Father God, who sees us as without fault. In this truth, joy overcomes us. We rejoice in his grace, mercy, and forgiveness. All praise to him.

The second passage of praise likewise overflows with astounding significance. In this praise to the only God our Savior, we adore him, acknowledging his glory, majesty, power, and authority.

Let's consider each one so we can amplify our comprehension of God's amazing, praise-worthy character:

- His glorious nature reminds us he is worthy of our honor, praise, and adoration.
- His majestic nature reflects his supreme

authority and sovereign rule. He is all-powerful.
- God's power transcends physical strength to embrace his supernatural prowess. He is omnipotent. No one is higher than him.
- God has the ultimate authority, more so than anyone else. He enforces laws, expects obedience, and judges. In this, we stand in awe. As such, we listen to his commands and desire to obey him.

This is what it means to ascribe to him all glory, majesty, power, and authority. This all comes to us through our Lord and Savior, Jesus.

Before time began, he was. He lives now. And we will be with him for all eternity. Jesus exists past, present, and future.

What can we learn from this passage about who God is? How should we respond?

[Discover more about praising God in Luke 19:37–40, Revelation 4:8, and Revelation 5:12–14.]

If you liked *James & Jude Bible Study*, please leave a review online. Your review will help others discover this book and encourage them to read it too. Thank you.

BOOKS IN THE 40-DAY BIBLE STUDY SERIES

Which book do you want to read next in the 40-Day Bible Study Series?

- Dear Theophilus (the Gospel of **Luke**, formerly *That You May Know*)
- Dear Theophilus, **Acts** (formerly *Tongues of Fire*)
- Dear Theophilus, **Isaiah** (formerly *For Unto Us*)
- Dear Theophilus, **Minor Prophets** (formerly *Return to Me*)
- Dear Theophilus, **Job** (formerly *I Hope in Him*)
- Living Water (**John**)

Books in the 40-Day Bible Study Series

- Love Is Patient (**1 and 2 Corinthians**)
- A New Heaven and a New Earth (**Revelation**)
- Love One Another (**1, 2, and 3 John**)
- Run with Perseverance (**Hebrews**)

FOR SMALL GROUPS, SUNDAY SCHOOL, AND CLASSES

James & Jude Bible Study makes an ideal eight-week Bible study discussion guide for small groups, Sunday School, and classes. To prepare for the conversation, read one chapter of this book each weekday, Monday through Friday.

- Week 1: read 1 through 5.
- Week 2: read 6 through 10.
- Week 3: read 11 through 15.
- Week 4: read 16 through 20.
- Week 5: read 21 through 25.
- Week 6: read 26 through 30.
- Week 7: read 31 through 35.
- Week 8: read 36 through 40.

For Small Groups, Sunday School, and Classes

When you get together, discuss the questions at the end of each chapter. The leader can use all the questions to guide this discussion or pick which ones to focus on.

Before beginning the discussion, pray as a group. Ask for Holy Spirit insight and clarity.

As you consider each chapter's questions:

- Look for how this can grow your understanding of the Bible.
- Evaluate how this can expand your faith perspective.
- Consider what you need to change in how you live your lives.

End by asking God to help apply what you've learned.

May God bless you as you read and study his Word.

IF YOU'RE NEW TO THE BIBLE

Each entry in this book contains Bible references. These can guide you if you want to learn more. If you're not familiar with the Bible, here's an overview to get you started, give some context, and minimize confusion.

First, the Bible is a collection of works written by various authors over several centuries. Think of the Bible as a diverse anthology of godly communication. It contains historical accounts, poetry, songs, letters of instruction and encouragement, messages from God sent through his representatives, and prophecies.

Most versions of the Bible have sixty-six books grouped into two sections: The Old Testament and the New Testament. The Old Testament contains

If You're New to the Bible

thirty-nine books that precede and anticipate Jesus. The New Testament includes twenty-seven books and covers Jesus's life and the work of his followers.

The reference notations in the Bible, such as Romans 3:23, are analogous to line numbers in a Shakespearean play. They serve as a study aid. Since the Bible is much longer and more complex than a play, its reference notations are more involved.

As already mentioned, the Bible is an amalgam of books, or sections, such as Genesis, Psalms, John, Acts, or 1 Peter. These are the names given to them, over time, based on the piece's author, audience, or purpose.

In the 1200s, each book was divided into chapters, such as Acts 2 or Psalm 23. In the 1500s, the chapters were further subdivided into verses, such as John 3:16. Let's use this as an example.

The name of the book (John) appears first, followed by the chapter number (3), a colon, and then the verse number (16). Sometimes called a chapter-verse reference notation, this helps people quickly find a specific text regardless of their version of the Bible.

Although the goal was to place these chapter and verse divisions at logical breaks, they sometimes

If You're New to the Bible

seem arbitrary. Therefore, it's good practice to read what precedes and follows each passage you're studying. The text before or after it may contain relevant insights into the portion you're exploring.

Here's how to look up a specific passage in the Bible based on its reference: Most Bibles contain a table of contents, which gives the page number for the beginning of each book. Start there. Locate the book you want to read, and turn to that page. Then flip forward to the chapter you want. Last, skim that chapter to locate the specific verse.

If you want to read online, enter the reference into BibleGateway.com or BibleHub.com. Also check out the YouVersion app.

Learn more about the greatest book ever written at ABibleADay.com, which provides a Bible blog, summaries of the books of the Bible, a dictionary of Bible terms, Bible reading plans, and other resources.

ABOUT PETER DEHAAN

Peter DeHaan, PhD, wants to change the world one word at a time. His books and blog posts discuss God, the Bible, and church, geared toward spiritual seekers and church dropouts. Many people feel church has let them down, and Peter seeks to encourage them as they search for a place to belong.

But he's not afraid to ask tough questions or make religious people squirm. He's not trying to be provocative. Instead, he seeks truth, even if it makes people uncomfortable. Peter urges Christians to push past the status quo and reexamine how they practice their faith in every part of their lives.

Peter earned his doctorate, awarded with high distinction, from Trinity College of the Bible and Theological Seminary. He lives with his wife in beautiful Southwest Michigan and wrangles crossword puzzles in his spare time.

A lifelong student of Scripture, Peter wrote the 1,000-page website ABibleADay.com to encourage people to explore the Bible, the greatest book ever written. His popular blog, at PeterDeHaan.com, addresses biblical Christianity to build a faith that matters.

Read his blog, receive his newsletter, and learn more at PeterDeHaan.com.

BOOKS BY PETER DEHAAN

40-Day Bible Study Series

Dear Theophilus (the Gospel of Luke, formerly *That You May Know*)

Dear Theophilus, Acts (formerly *Tongues of Fire*)

Dear Theophilus, Isaiah (formerly *For Unto Us*)

Dear Theophilus, Minor Prophets (formerly *Return to Me*)

Dear Theophilus, Job (formerly *I Hope in Him*)

Living Water (the Gospel of John)

Love Is Patient (Paul's letters to the Corinthians)

A New Heaven and a New Earth (John's Revelation)

Love One Another (John's letters)

Run with Perseverance (the book of Hebrews)

Holiday Celebration Bible Study Series

The Advent of Jesus (an Advent devotional)

The Ministry of Jesus (an Ordinary Time devotional)

The Passion of Jesus (a Lenten devotional)

The Victory of Jesus (an Easter devotional)

Bible Character Sketches Series

Women of the Bible

The Friends and Foes of Jesus

Old Testament Sinners and Saints

More Old Testament Sinners and Saints

Heroes and Heavies of the Apocrypha

Visiting Churches Series

Shopping for Church

Visiting Online Church

52 Churches

The 52 Churches Workbook

More Than 52 Churches

The More Than 52 Churches Workbook

Other Books

Jesus's Broken Church

Martin Luther's 95 Theses

The Christian Church's LGBTQ Failure

Bridging the Sacred-Secular Divide

Beyond Psalm 150

How Big Is Your Tent?

For the latest list of all Peter's books, go to PeterDeHaan.com/books.